THE CULT EXPERIENCE

THE CULT EXPERIENCE

An Overview of Cults, Their Traditions and Why People Join Them

By

JOHN J. COLLINS, PH.D.

CHARLES C THOMAS • PUBLISHER
Springfield • Illinois • U.S.A.

Published and Distributed Throughout the World by

CHARLES C THOMAS • PUBLISHER
2600 South First Street
Springfield, Illinois 62794-9265

© *1991 by* CHARLES C THOMAS • PUBLISHER

ISBN 0-398-05721-4

Library of Congress Catalog Card Number: 90-49591

Printed in the United States of America
SC-R-3

Library of Congress Cataloging-in-Publication Data

Collins, John J. (John James), 1938–
    The cult experience : an overview of cults, their traditions, and
why people form them / by John J. Collins.
        p.   cm.
    Includes bibliographical references and index.
    ISBN 0-398-05721-4
    1. Cults—United States—History—20th century.   2. United States—
Religion—1960–   3. Cults.   I. Title.
BL2525.C63   1991
291—dc20   90-49591
                                                                                          CIP

PREFACE

Religious cults have attracted the attention of religious leaders, politicians, young persons and their anxious parents, as well as seekers of truth in general. Attitudes towards such organizations range from their being recognized as works of the Devil to feelings that they represent a long overdue expression of religious vitality. Knowledge concerning cults, accurate or otherwise, thus find a large, if diverse, audience. There is also a large and increasingly expanding literature on cults. This literature can leave a person who wishes to gain a little general insight into the cult phenomenon very bewildered. Much of the writing on cults has also been done either from a narrow point of view, pro or con, or from a scholarly perspective, with footnotes and asides that may be a bit beyond the curious reader.

This book is intended to be a short introduction to the cult experience and it deals very briefly with a number of major topics of interest. It begins with a definition of religion in its various dimensions and presents the religious groups that occur as types of religious expressions. Cults are then defined as one such expression and from a number of points of view. A composite definition is presented at the end of the book. Three cults that were typical of American groups in the 1960s (Scientology, the Hare Krishna, and the Divine Light Mission) are briefly presented to give supporting materials for points raised later in the text.

Several chapters detail who joins cults and what the lure of such religious expressions appears to be. Various reasons for joining cults are given both on the theoretical level and with reference to specific cult groups, including descriptive materials on other cults in the United States. The process of conversion—how one becomes a member—is also discussed. Models for conversion as well as specific cult techniques such as "love bombing" among the Moonies (i.e. the Unification Church) are included, along with responses by the families of cult members to such involvements. A consideration is also made of the origins of cults and the stages that mark the typical careers of such new religions. Why are some cults more successful and more lasting than others? Factors that encourage or limit cult growth are considered. Finally, along such theoretical lines, various schemes for the classification of cults are discussed so the reader becomes aware of how very different cults may be from each other.

Cults are also examined in time and space. Native American and other groups are examined in the United States and the Caribbean, including the Ghost Dance and Peyotism, Santeria and the Ras Tafari. Descriptions such as these are continued with examples derived from the Pacific, Africa, and Asia, including such groups as Cargo cults, the Jamaa Movement, Perfect Liberty, and others from Japan. Finally, consideration is made of how cults may be evaluated as legitimate forms of religious expression.

All of the information is presented in a brief and non-technical manner and requires no special background by the reader, except for interest on cults. Bibliographic Essays are included at the back of the book which give fuller accounts of all the materials presented and sources for further study.

J.J.C.

CONTENTS

THE CULT EXPERIENCE

Chapter 1

THE CONCEPT OF CULTS

The religious landscape in the United States has been the scene of shifts and changes since the early days of our nation. It has never been monochromatic in nature. Change has been very marked since the late fifties, marked by the rise of a number of new religions. These are the "cult phenomenon" commented on by many people. Modern media has perhaps made us more aware of these than we were even a few generations ago, and recognition and study of them by academic scholars has also brought them to our attention. Claims have been made that more than six hundred new religions have been created or imported here in the last few decades and their sheer numbers alone have perhaps polarized commentators into opposing camps. Some writers—generally anti-cult—consider them bogus religions and to be a source of danger to their members and to society in general. Other writers have suggested that such a flourishing of new faiths highlights a new kind of religious awareness or consciousness, particularly among young people. As is often the case, the truth may lie somewhere between these extremes or may be different in the case of each cult.

What is a cult? How does one define them as subject matter for a book? I believe it is best if we start at a more fundamental level and examine the basic nature of religion. Religion is the most special aspect of human culture. It sets us apart from other animals and can be traced as far back as the Old Stone Age. Precisely what it is that religion represents is difficult to define. Different scholars and fields of inquiry offer different definitions. Clearly, however, religion represents an attempt on the part of most members of our species to transform themselves to some kind of higher level of existence, to gain enlightenment or salvation. Religions assume that a more powerful and authentic reality exists and offers ways to bring the individual into contact with it, or at least to have some sort of relations with that reality. The focus of religion may be comprised of some deity or deities or may be represented by some more abstract concept. The rituals and other activities that bring such a relation into

3

existence reflect the thought that we are unable to reach our full potential as humans unless we take this reality into account. They suggest that there is a world of special things, the sacred, beyond our everyday existence, the world of secular reality. In this sense, religion is the attempt to experience the sacred realm of being.

Religion, however conceived, is expressed in a number of ways that we will want to consider as we look at cults. Any system of religion (particular faith) will have a mental level consisting of beliefs, doctrines, myths, values, ethics, and related concepts. What god is worshipped, the relation of deity to humans, and the benefits to be gained from relationship to it are all questions that must be conceptualized in religious systems. Second are the rituals themselves; the religious practices or expressions that create or maintain our desired relation to the sacred. Sacrifices and other worship activities constitute a very visible and tangible dimension of religious behavior. Finally, there is a social aspect. This is the interaction between the believers/worshippers. This involves not only taking one another into account—as between leaders and followers—but deals with how the individual worshipper defines him or herself in relation to the higher reality. Some people desire personal encounter, a kind of "one on one" with the supernatural. Particular faiths may emphasize such experience. Other people feel ethics to be primary. They want to live according to principles derived from or defined by the higher reality. For them, a life in accord with "cosmic law" becomes primary and some faiths may emphasize this relation. Perhaps a majority of people enjoin the coming together of adherents in group rituals, thus collectively worshipping what they feel they could not experience directly. In this way they seek salvation, even active aid from the sacred world.

Cults will be seen to be a reflection of what has been said about religion. They are a type of expression along these lines. They are not, however, the only form assumed by religion. Two other better known forms of religious expression are churches and sects. These are "bread and butter" topics in most sociology books on religion, although, unfortunately, no consensus exists as to their specific definitions. Usually they are compared in ideal terms. The church is an established mainline religious organization. It is therefore a respectable part of a society like the United States and represents the religious status quo—with an interest in and a sharing of the values and other aspects of the surrounding secular world. Generally, the church represents a large group of people and has a formal structure existing on a number of levels down to the local congregation. Relatively clear rules define doctrine and ritual, ethics and the interpersonal relations of members. Those who belong are usually in a church because their parents were members or because of living in a geographical region serviced by that faith. They are born into the church. Rituals and other activities in churches tend to be restrained and follow traditional sets of routines not generally given to easy manipulation or experimentation.

Sects, ideally, represent smaller religious associations which are often begun as protest movements within established churches. Founders and adherents often seek more purity of doctrine or the expression of more genuine religious feelings. As a result the behavior of members may be less restrained and more emotional. Organization may be less formal and with fewer levels than in churches. Membership in sects is heavily voluntary; one has to make a decision to join and undergo a conversion process or experience. Sects are usually not mainline faiths that share most of society's values. They are more withdrawn from society and may even be actively opposed to it.

Despite these ideal characters, there are overlaps in church and sect characters. Some scholars have suggested that the single most useful distinction between these organizations follows the relation they each have to the secular world, to society itself. A church accepts the social environment in which it exists and the sect rejects that social environment! This is not a total contrast. One should think of a pure church at one extreme with the pure sect at the other. Most organizations will fall somewhere on a line between one type or the other. If people in a religious group have different rules and values than those of society in general (e.g. no smoking or drinking), if they see themselves as specially enlightened or righteous (non-members are of less value as persons), and if they attempt to remain apart (psychologically or residentially) from society, then they fall towards the sect end of the scale. Sociologically speaking, they exist in a state of tension with their surrounding social environment. As they experience less tension in these respects they fall towards the church ideal.

What then is a cult? How does it fit in with the above contrast between church and sect? Authorities are not in agreement and there are many differing definitions. These are based in part on what aspect of a cult one wishes to emphasize. A definition in terms of structure will emphasize authority and organization. A definition based on function will stress what the cult hopes to accomplish or what scholars see as their effects.

Which cults one uses as a sample can also bias classification and definition. Rather than a mere recitation of definitions, we can look at some of the characteristics that are often considered as typically part of cults. Perhaps in the last chapter, with considerable theory and description behind us, we can hazard a definition along with an evaluation of this religious phenomena. For the present we can offer three sets of characteristics to help as a comparison to other religious groups. Further lists of characters are to be found in the Bibliographic Essays at the end of this book.

Willa Appel, an anthropologist, has suggested that cults share four major attributes. First, she believes they have an authoritarian structure. Leaders, gurus, prophets, whatever, make decisions as to the beliefs and behaviors of lay persons or ordinary members who are less gifted with the truth. Such members have to accept the authority of their "spiritual betters." Sometimes the authority is formal in a hierarchial fashion, other times it is more personal; no one stands between the leader/founder and those who follow. We shall examine situations of each of these types in later chapters.

A second character is the regimentation of followers in cults. Members, it is suggested by Appel, often dress alike, talk alike, think alike. If you have seen one Hare Krishna, you have seen them all! There is clearly a cult "party line" rigidly insisted upon that promotes this, and in recruiting new members this becomes helpful as well. Whether this is a really different aspect for cults as opposed to churches and sects could be debated. Party lines are a character of most religious groups that have any organizational tightness. Certainly the character of authority also overlaps with sects so neither of these two attributes provides clear characterization.

A third characteristic of cults is their renunciation of the world. Leader and member alike generally see the secular societies in which they exist as corrupt, evil, the work of Satan and view their own rejection and avoidance of the mainstream as necessary both to join the cult and to maintain or gain the purity needed to pursue their religious goals. In this respect, cults stand like sects in tension with society and so are opposite from churches. Appel's fourth point follows somewhat from this, a belief that only members of the cult are gifted with the truth. Only they know the nature of and best relations to the higher reality that promises salvation or aid in life. Other faiths and of course secular/scientific views are bogus in these respects. Again, this is very true of cults, but one can find such a view in churches and sects as well; in fact in many types of groups. I remember my army experiences only too vividly!

Appel believes that three other attitudes are derived from these main characters. She holds that an attitude of moral superiority prevails in cults, not only the truth but a feeling that what members do is right or correct under any circumstances; secular laws count for less. More than one writer has commented on how cult members may misrepresent themselves in recruitment activities and in raising funds and feel no moral doubts since what they do has higher meaning. There may be more of this attitude among cultists, but I am sure that there are more than traces of it in other religious groups. Another attitude she calls rigidity of thought; an unwillingness, perhaps even inability, to think in non-cult terms. This has often been observed by those who study cults and sometimes is ascribed to brainwashing procedures applied to cult converts. We will tackle this issue in a later chapter.

Finally, there is the derived attitude of dimunition of regard for the individual. Cults exist to promote goals beyond any individual and leaders may "use" members to accomplish those ends. Members exist, as it were, for the greater good and can be worked long hours at recruiting, fund raising, building or whatever and then given inadequate food and rest and housing in return. Some kinds of cults surely manipulate members in these respects. It is also true at times, as many casual observers have remarked, that leaders will put their own needs for fleets of cars, grand residences and the like above even the goals of the cult and misuse its members in their efforts to become wealthy. This is probably more typical of cults than of other religious groups, although it must be said that the role of a missionary in any faith may be less than a life of comfort. At any rate, Appel sees these several characters or attributes as one way to conceptualize the nature of cults. Other writers have also mentioned these in their definitions.

J. Milton Yinger is a sociologist. He has listed a set of cult characteristics and we can examine his views on this topic. Some of his characters have already been considered. Cults, he says, represent a sharp break with society and have (or at least were begun by) a dominant leader, a person with great personal force or charisma. Yinger also feels that cults lack organizational structure in being more like sects than churches in this regard. This is true only of some cults! He contributes a really key character in saying that cults are heavily involved in a search for mystical experiences, what we called earlier a personal encounter with higher realities. In this, cults again seem closer to sects than churches as a type of religious organization. We shall examine many modern and tribal examples both of this cult tendency. Related to this, their emotionalism is sect-like as well.

Yinger points out that cults are often small in size, shortlived in their careers, and often of local character. These are probably true characters if we take into account any large sample of cults from both modern and tribal societies. Many have only a few hundred core members, they often fade away after the death of their founder, and may not spread very far from the point of their organization. We will examine cases that demonstrate all of these situations. On the other hand, some cults have followers in the hundreds of thousands. Some have long careers spanning many generations of members and some are nearly worldwide in distribution. On balance, though, they seem to be more "sectish" in at least some of these respects.

Finally, among other characters, this author suggests that cults mainly concern themselves with problems of the individual rather than with those of the larger world. The convert to a cult is seeking his or her own salvation to problems, is seeking salvation or enlightenment. This is certainly true. We will examine many specific individualized motives for joining these groups in Chapter 3. It is also true, however, that this is a reality both of emphasis and degree. Some cults are more concerned with saving the world or building a better society than with the lesser needs of any individual. Utopias transcend individuals. Yet, in either case, cults do not accept the status quo, they are not akin to churches in these regards, although churches do of course exist for individual salvational needs. Comparison does become confusing. Let's examine the views of one more expert on cults.

Robert S. Ellwood, Jr. comes from a tradition of religious studies on the general level rather than examination of religion from a purely anthropological or sociological view. He has also written on many orthodox religions. In his view cults represent attempts along rather mystical lines to gain ecstatic experiences. These are states of extreme emotional excitement: "highs" in today's idiom. In this respect they remind us of primitive shamans and their altered states of consciousness. The difference, however, is that the tribal shaman and his or her followers are the religion of society, whereas cult leaders as modern shamans represent a non-orthodox and often withdrawn membership group.

This general perspective stimulates Ellwood to suggest fifteen characters for cults which I will merge together in a somewhat different order. I omit those already covered in other schemes. Clearly, one character of importance is the presence of a founder or leader who has ecstatic abilities or at least a strong interest in them. Along with this is his or her ability to induce them in others or use them for the benefit of followers. Charisma is integral to such persons and their behavior. There may be supernatural beings associated who also give aid to the followers. Healing—an element of shamanism—may also occur along with the presence of magical techniques. All of these presume at least some use of what we would designate as psychic powers. Members may also participate in such behaviors as chanting, dancing, meditation or other acts designed to raise emotional levels. In short, cults are usually not passive affairs but involve active involvement of devotees or followers. The ecstatic aspects of cults are not lost or subordinated as is often the case in mainline religions!

Other cult characteristics in this scheme fall along different lines. Ellwood suggests that they do represent a reaction to orthodoxy in the societies in which they occur. They differ from the religious establishment and are often very critical of it. They also combine eclecticism and syncretism; that is, they often draw beliefs, practices and inspiration from many sources and integrate these often very different aspects of behavior together. Truthfully, in some cases they appear to outsiders as a kind of "junkyard of the supernatural," although to members who view them as a final truth they obviously represent perfection. Cults have, with respect to this perfection, a kind of optimism. Cults have a sense that their practices can produce benefits. If such benefits are not to be experiences in the here and now, then they will surely be available in some better world to come. Finally, among other traits not omitted in the present summary, Ellwood feels that cults generally provide an easy process for gaining membership since their stock in trade (like sects) is to recruit most or all of their members from the outside. To highlight conversion they often require a definite act of separation for converts in this process; what many writers call the "bridge-burning" act. This often makes it difficult to sever ties to the cult even if one becomes disillusioned with the value of continued membership. Ellwood adds that in some cases a sacred center of sorts is set up as headquarters for the leader or as a place of mythic or other significance. This may function as a stimulus for pilgrimages or related activities by group members.

Cults surely have many characteristics. Just as obviously, the lists provided by different writers overlap in some cases and diverge in others. Some highlight aspects such as control, as in the case of Appel, others emotional experiences as do Yinger and Ellwood. The reader senses that they are in fact talking about the same phenomenon, but chooses to examine it and thus define it from different perspectives. They also use traits or characters of different magnitude and significance. The presence of ecstatic or mystical experiences surely is on a different level of relevance than the existence of a sacred center or the fact that members may see themselves as specially gifted with the truth. So how do we define cults as a form of religious expression? How do we draw lines around them? As previously mentioned, we will wait on this matter until the last chapter, until we have descriptive materials both from modern and tribal peoples as data. Perhaps by then we will have uncovered their essential nature. It is clear, however, that cults will fall on our church-sect tension scale toward the end represented by sects and perhaps heavily towards that end. Cults do differ from sects, however, in one very fundamental manner: sects develop out of churches. They represent a kind of renewal attempt, whether it be more purity of doctrine, ritual, or ordinary behavior. They are something new within an established tradition. Cults involve innovation. Whatever purity or other aspects of behavior they espouse they are not connected to the traditional religious systems of their societies. They represent something new from without—either by originating a new religion locally or by importing it from some other society as in the case of so many Eastern cults in the United States today. Such a notion relative to cults must surely be a part of their definition. To add further characteristics we need to turn to data. Consider which of the traits suggested in this chapter seem to be important in the three cults described in the next chapter.

Chapter 2

THREE AMERICAN CULTS

In this chapter we shall examine three religious organizations that we can use to typify the cult experience in the United States. Selection is somewhat arbitrary here. Our purpose is to provide some descriptive material that can be referred to when we talk about various aspects of cults in coming chapters and to see the definitional character of cults come alive. Later chapters will also include descriptive material but in less complete detail than what is supplied here. In those chapters material is used to highlight or exemplify particular ideas. I have selected as our three examples: Scientology, the Hare Krsnas, and the Divine Light Mission.

Scientology

Scientology, or as members would have it, the Church of Scientology, is the handywork of Lafayette Ronald Hubbard. Details on the life of this "prophet" are somewhat obscure, perhaps intentionally so. He was born in Nebraska around 1911 and spent much time traveling about the world including the Far East where his father was stationed in the navy. He himself was in the navy during World War II. He has at one time or another claimed to have accomplished many things, for example, field work in anthropology. These are difficult to verify! He did write excellent science fiction and after a lapse of many years he recently returned to this genre. Detractors often call his cult the science fiction religion. He died recently.

The origins of the cult called Scientology can be traced back to a movement he began in the late fourties called Dianetics. Possibly the first public article on this appeared in 1950 in *Astounding Science Fiction* magazine whose editor felt that dianetic techniques had cured him of a chronic ailment. Somewhat later that year a book, *Dianetics: The Modern Science of Mental Health,* was published and Hubbard went on a lecture tour to acquaint the public with his discoveries along these lines. A foundation was created for dianetic studies. The message of his book and lectures seems to have had an instant appeal as a therapy technique for a variety of mental and other problems. It was also a "quick fix" type of therapy compared to mainline psychological techniques.

The theory and practice of Dianetics is rather complex. Briefly, however, the following notions are involved. Dianetics concerns itself with the removal of what are called *engrams.* Engrams are "psychic" scars in our mind that prevent our full adult potential from developing. They make us less than we could be in a fashion similar to repressions in Freudian psychological thinking. Like Freud, Hubbard conceives of our mind as operating on a number of levels. Our conscious mind (analytic mind) operates to process incoming data in a computer-type fashion. It takes in data and forms decisions about actions. We also have a kind of unconscious mind (reactive mind) which also records our experiences. Unlike the analytic level which shuts down in stress situations, this level of mind continues to record those experiences and forms engrams. These then cause problems—like neuroses for Freud—inhibiting our full potential as human beings until they are removed.

Removal of engrams is accomplished by *auditing,* again somewhat like psychoanalysis. This involves a Dianetics practitioner and consists of questions and answers with an auditee along with responses, subtle and otherwise, which can bring the engrams to the surface and expose them. Such an experience apparently clears up their negative effects; awareness is mastery or so it would seem! Dianetics rather parts company with traditional psychoanalysis at this point. The latter takes clients back into childhood experiences. Hubbard's auditing techniques take the client back to engrams formed as a fetus in the womb. Ultimately, the goal of a number of auditing sessions is for a person to have all of his or her engrams removed, to reach, in Hubbard's terms, a state of "clear." Reaching such a state should surely produce superhumans and in the early fifties some "clears" did claim accomplishments, although verification of them appears not to have been forthcoming.

Dianetics began to spread as a movement along with its message of quick hopes for a better functioning person. Unfortunately for the master therapist, however, anyone who purchased his book or was cleared by someone else could use its techniques and set up shop as a therapist. They could practice with their own clients and even add some of their own ideas to the development of Dianetics. Heretic therapists began to emerge and Hubbard began to lose control over his own movement. It should also be added that the professional psychological fraternity was not accepting of this new therapy and much criticism was directed against it. Finally, as is the case in many movements of the self-help variety, interest had begun to wane in the mid-fifties.

Hubbard, or L. Ron as he is affectionately known to his disciples, had to deal with these problems and he managed to do so by resorting to a number of expedients. On one level he reasserted some degree of control by requiring the licensing of practitioners; auditors had to go through him for proper credentials. Better than this, however, he took his basic movement and by adding layers of new elements turned it into a real religious cult, the cult we know today as Scientology. This cult adds a supernatural ingredient and ever more complex levels of mental or spiritual health. Additional criteria for membership led to the consolidation of the Church of Scientology in 1955.

We can examine two of these new dimensions. The most crucial and cult element is the concept of the *thetan* which Hubbard developed based on auditing his own life and past lives! The thetan is our own individual consciousness which not only can create our external reality but has the ability to separate from our body and mind. How can this be done? It turns out that what we conceive of as consciousness is really an essence of an immortal celestial being. These beings existed millions of years ago and for some purpose entered into human bodies. Ultimately, they forgot their supernatural origins, failed to recall who they really were, and in an amnesia context became trapped in a reincarnating series of human bodies. Just to be clear in a situation such as this is not sufficient. We must go beyond clear to what Hubbard calls the level of *operating thetan.* This means we are cleared not only of present engrams but those of past lives as well. To look at it from our thetan point of view, Scientology can overcome the illusion that these thetans have that they are human! When one becomes an operating thetan the amnesia regarding origins is gone. We become aware of our own true supernatural nature and become independent of anything in this world. We can be in the world but independent of it. We can be the gods we once were!

All this obviously requires better auditing techniques than in Dianetics if we are to achieve the goal in any reasonable amount of time. This leads to a second new element, an electrical device known as the E-meter. This little machine can aid here, in that it supposedly measures areas of tension when an auditee responds to verbal and other stimuli. This allows the auditor to explore this tension and get to the engram behind it more rapidly. All this being valuable, it is natural to seek perfection and wish superhuman powers, how does one get involved in Scientology?

A person begins his or her career in Scientology by purchasing mail-order lessons. These are copyrighted and packaged in small portions and are expensive. After one accepts these preliminary ideas, a person can go to a local unit of the organization, an "org" in scientological terms, for clearing by certified auditors and further instruction in doctrines. It should be added at this point that this series of organizations developed after Hubbard went to England in 1959 and set up a centralized control structure with a finance division, certification division, and the like to which local orgs remain subservient. There are also ethics officers that insure fidelity of beliefs and loyalties. If a member has relatives or friends who are not sympathetic, these officers force one to "disconnect" from them.

The next step is to join with the local group more closely and pursue training as an auditor and help spread cult doctrines—ultimately to help clear the entire planet. After a probationary period of anywhere from six months to two years one comes to identify one's own goals with those of the movement, at which point (as in all cults described in this book) it becomes more difficult to doubt the truth of Scientology teachings. The whole process is time consuming. One has to work one's way not only up to operating thetan, but Hubbard has defined seven or eight levels or "techs" of this state that one has to pass through. Many of these seem added so that no one approaches too closely to the leader himself. And these are expensive lessons. Data on the Los Angeles org from 1979 indicates the following costs in rough estimates: $3,700 for a solo audit course, almost $1,800 for a "grade six" release that follows it, and $2,900 for a clearing course. For fifty hours of training beyond clear the cost is $12,700 and for operating thetan processing, $16,000. Salvation thus requires a steady and considerable financial commitment.

Hubbard "resigned" from active leadership in 1966 so he could work on new doctrine. He took up residence on a boat in the Mediterranean with the *Sea Org* and the inner nucleus of the Scientology movement. With his recent death it will be interesting to see what events occur in the future of this cult. It is interesting that his recent science fiction writing sold well enough to lead to the more prominent resurfacing of his *Dianetics* book in bookstores. It may well be that the cult will recycle back to earlier levels.

Hare Krsna

The founder of this cult is A. C. Bhaktivedanta Swami Prabhupada, born Abhay Cheran De in Calcutta, India in 1896. The title Bhaktivedanta refers to devotion to a body of Hindu religious literature. Prabhupada means "one at whose feet many masters sit." It pays to advertise! Acb as he will be called here joined a Hindu sect rather late in life. This sect, founded by the guru Caitanya, differed from mainline Hinduism of the devotional school in worshipping the god Krsna as a separate supernatural being rather than as an incarnation (avatar) of the god Visnu. Despite Acb's advanced years, his spiritual progress was such that he was ordered to take this faith to the Western world and so at age seventy he came to the United States in 1965. The next year he founded the International Society for Krsna Consciousness (Iskon), the true name for this movement. In 1970 he founded a governing body for Iskon with managers for world regions and lesser leaders, including an advanced order of special missionaries, right down to local temple leaders with authority over local devotees. At the high point of this movement here there may have been more than eighty such local organizations.

The founder himself remained the supreme authority figure, although in recent years before his death he rarely interacted with ordinary cult members. He was worshipped as the latest in a long line of leaders tracing back to the earthly appearance of the god Krsna thousands of years ago. As such, he is not a god as are some cult leaders, but he was Krsna's representative on earth and a mediator with that deity.

What does this cult believe? What are its techniques for salvation? Hare Krsna ideology goes back to a classic work of Indian religious thinking, the song of god, Bhagavad Gita. This work helped to found the emphasis on devotionalism in Hinduism, called *Bhakti.* It established the notion that the love of humans for God will be reciprocated in God's love for humans and that God can save his devotees. The more sectarian writing, the Bhagavatam, explores more specifically the worship of forms of Krsna and the devotion of one's whole being in surrender to Krsna. Iskon represents an attempt to raise people's consciousness to the level of God. We forget, as it were, that we were eternally related to Krsna, that our soul is eternal. Because of our ignorance we are reborn over and over again into a succession of human bodies—a common Eastern conception. We identify with our present body rather than with Krsna and we must overcome this falsehood. We must realize Krsna consciousness, realize our relation to this deity and that everything, including life, comes from him. Therefore, we must give our life in service to him and constantly think of him. Once our consciousness is so raised we will gain release from the cycle of rebirth and our soul can resume its spiritual existence with Krsna.

One accomplishes the above, of course, by joining a local Iskon temple. Once one makes this commitment, the most common act is the "great chanting," the maha mantra, a recitation that is repeated many times each day under various circumstances.

> Hare Krsna Hare Krsna
> Krsna Krsna Hare Hare
> Hare Rama Hare Rama
> Rama Rama Hare Hare

Hare means the supreme pleasure and energy potency of Lord Krsna, and Rama is another of his names. So one begins an Iskon career by chanting and by observing basic temple rules. These rules include a prohibition on gambling which is extended to mean a ban on games and on non-religious activities. Even talking about things not related to Krsna is frowned upon! There is also a rule against intoxicants—booze, drugs, coffee, even medicines. This may in fact be valuable for former drug users who often join this cult. No immoral sex is permitted and for that matter apparently hardly any other. One can marry if convinced it is the will of Krsna or join as a married couple, but sex apparently is very limited. Certainly, it could interfere with constant thoughts of Krsna. Naturally, men and women, married or not, sleep separately. Dietary taboos are also in evidence, with a prohibition on meat, fish, and eggs, among other things. As we shall see presently, eating is itself an act of worship and so is severely constrained.

Rules such as the above give to this cult the regimented character discussed in Chapter 1. They certainly test the ability of the new member to endure the difficulties of group living enjoined by this cult. If one is male, one also shaves his head save for a lock of hair and wears a long, draped garment. Women wear saris, traditional Indian female clothing. All devotees carry a string of prayer beads for keeping track of maha mantra recitations among other things plus other paraphernalia that immediately single them out as cult members. Such devices are signs of their new and hopeful status as seekers of Krsna consciousness. Of course, property is given up upon entrance and personal possessions severely limited. If one is successful in these things, after about six months one can declare one's membership to be in the nature of a lifetime commitment and then take a new (spiritual) name. After another period of about the same duration one passes through an initiation, receiving a sacred thread to wear and a secret mantra of one's own. This raises the dedicated devotee to the level of Brahman priest. Such a person as a full member can now aspire to a leadership position and perform cult rites for other members.

The setting for such a progression is an Iskon temple, or ashram. This, at least in the past, was an older, large house locally purchased by the cult. Its largest room is given over to worship activities by setting up a large altar there, generally a solid platform (stage-like) usually of marble on which sit large statues of Krsna and related cult deities, flowers, incense burners, pictures of the guruline and other paraphernalia. At the opposite end of the room there is a chair symbolically reserved for the use of the guru. In this holy atmosphere various ritual activities are enacted.

The basic Hare Krsna ritual is the aratrika, which is done to please Krsna and also to enhance the feelings of members regarding him. Unless the day is entirely devoted to special rites, this is performed up to six times. A leader begins by chanting a prayer in Sanskrit and then the devotees, accompanied by music, join in as well. The maha mantra is chanted to the accompanyment of a simple shuffling dance. The chant grows in volume and exhuberance and the dance becomes very animated, opening up at least some members to an ecstatic state. Formal offerings also occur. A leader, pujari, brings covered food trays and places them on the altar with much ritualistic maneuvering. She offers a prayer and allows Krsna to "eat" for about fifteen minutes and then removes the plates.

Incense offerings are waved in front of the statues, and flowers and other objects are added to the altar. The pujari blows on a conch shell (like Krsna's mythic flute), the chanting stops and devotees recline on the floor for responsive prayers and shouts of "victory" for their spiritual aims. Water from the altar is sprinkled on everyone's head as a blessing. Food from the offering plates is transferred to those of cult members who partake of it and sometimes flowers are given to various devotees as an extra aid in the removal of sin. At the end of the first and last daily aratrika there is an additional special rite involving a sacred plant. This plant—tulasi—is believed to incarnate the essence of a female spirit/soul and thus is worshipped as a pure devotee of Krsna. Offerings are made by members who believe by so doing they can remove effects of their past sinful acts. The plant, which is kept in a special room and cared for by a special caretaker, is placed in the main worship room on a stand and members move around it while dancing and chanting to the accompaniment of a bell. Other special rites also occur.

Such ceremonies are high points in days which are lengthy and filled with other activities. Many members fail to adapt to the communal life-style and continuous devotion ethic. In the words of cult members, they become "bloopers" and leave the movement. Nevertheless, even a brief stay will ensure them a rebirth that will find Krsna consciousness. Those of us in the outside world, "karmi" will be much less fortunate. But it is difficult. A typical day in an ashram will begin at 3:30 A.M. for food, flower and other preparations and a 5:00 aratrika and classes at 6:00. At 8:45, breakfast ensues followed by upkeep activities. Later, some devotees leave for the streets to chant and beg for donations and distribute cult magazines.

It should be pointed out at this juncture that this is a rather financially solvent cult, though members themselves do not materially benefit. Devotees may request money from relatives and beg and sell magazines in the streets. The cult has its own publishing facilities (Iskon Press) and it also owns the Spiritual Sky Incense Company (sales of $2 million in 1974) which supplies their own needs plus commercial sales. Work on the streets is for Krsna, of course, and as well as raising money for expenses it provides (along with Sunday dinners), a medium for recruiting potential new members.

To continue our day, there is a noon worship rite and then more members take to the streets. At about 6:00 P.M. everyone returns for milk and cookies followed by another aratrika and classes. At 10:00 P.M. a time for rest is signified. It is small wonder that not all members make this life-style their spiritual career. Perhaps in recognition of this a recent cult development has been the Friends of Lord Krsna—a looser organization of persons who are encouraged to practice Krsna consciousness in their own homes and to merely visit the local temple, eventually becoming ready to accept the rules and other habits of full-time members. Such lay members are also accorded the title devotee.

Divine Light Mission

The Divine Light Mission is identified with Guru Maharaj Ji. During the heyday of this cult he was also referred to as the boy guru. Ji was born in India and raised in a family whose head, Sri Hans Ji Maharaj Ji, was also a leader of a cult. He grew up with the expectation that he and his brothers would display spiritual gifts. Certainly he was treated as special by his father's devotees and in fact he did manifest a capacity for meditating long hours as a young child. At age eight he was named to take his father's place, although his mother, "Holy Mother," and his eldest brother were the real powers behind his spiritual throne.

During the 1960s some Americans seeking new forms of spiritual awareness visited India in search of a guru and converted to Maharaj Ji's teachings, returning back to India in 1971 in the hopes he would bring the cult to the United States. At the tender age of thirteen and over Holy Mother's objections he did so, setting up a headquarters near Denver, Colorado. By 1973, considerable interest in his cult had developed with some fifty thousand individuals having been presented with its doctrines. Many members were only temporarily interested, however, using the cult as a way station to other cults and life-styles. Others subsequently became disenchanted as we shall see shortly. There were possibly less than 1200 fully committed members by 1977.

The belief system presented by this cult is that there exists a single reality of which we are all a part. God is this reality. Unlike the claims of many religions, Divine Light Mission holds that we can know God directly and quickly since as the source of all things God is really primordial energy — the Divine Light. God is the physicist's big bang as it were! In this sense all religions are true and the insight of God as the Divine Light substantiates all of them. In fact, Maharaj Ji has said that he really did not wish to found a new religion but to make more committed followers in those that already exist, for example, to make perfect Christians. Yet, "if you cannot find God in any other way, come to me." Cult teachings do provide an alternative, and a simple one at that, to orthodox, mainline faiths!

His active teachings consist in what is called *giving knowledge,* or a knowledge session. In this practice one can come to know God directly, a belief that certainly led to the great initial interest potential converts manifested towards this cult. More specifically, one is trained along with a few others at one time by a special cult member, a mahatma, to experience four events which give one the knowledge. Such a session is the experience of God. First, people are individually shown how to see an intense light within themselves and how to meditate on this in the future. This is God in light form—the Divine Light. Second, one is made aware of the sound of creation (music of the spheres) within oneself and is trained to listen for it in meditation. Third, one becomes aware of a "nectar" like butter and honey that flows in the body and how to taste this during meditation experiences. Lastly, one becomes aware of an internal vibration and is told to meditate on this at all times. This is said to be the name of God.

It is not entirely clear what actually occurs during a knowledge session in this cult. What does occur in general however is rather quick, ecstatic, and addictive, in that the convert wishes to recapture it over and over again. Though it seems not to occur later on with the same intensity, members still refer to it as being "blissed out." They do in fact feel that they have experienced God and they generally report a transformation of their lives; becoming more energetic in behavior, gaining a feeling that events in their lives are part of some larger plan, and that God is always with them, becoming manifest in their behavior. It should be mentioned at this point that some members believe the guru himself to be God or the tangible expression of this reality. Perhaps the more abstract concepts of the cult are too difficult for these members to understand. The results in improvement of life remain the same.

Where does one go from being blissed out in a knowledge session? One can attend satsang—the company of truth—after this, an informal discussion session among devotees concerning their improved life experiences. Devotees can also work for the guru and let the world know that such knowledge and help is available. In these respects there are two levels of cult involvement. One can join what is called a premie center. This is a communal household of devotees held together by their links to the cult. They live and work together and give 30 percent of their income to cult leaders. They have some rules like those of the Hare Krsna, but they are not too strict; married couples and children commonly reside here. On the other hand, ashrams are cooperative households who devote all their time and possessions to this cult. They are very much like those of the Krsnas since residents follow strict rules—no sex, meat and other foods, non-cult-related activities and the like. Residents must follow the direction of a leader appointed by the Denver headquarters. Commitment here is total.

What seems to have begun as a promising cult movement has essentially fizzled out at the present time and scholars have suggested two main reasons for this in addition to the idea that one can use this knowledge as the basis for just about anything spiritual without committing to active membership in the cult. First, the cult rented the Houston Astrodome in 1973 to hold a millennial festival. The guru was to give a knowledge session and members, many of whom believed his presence portended some new Age of Aquarius, had greatly raised expectations as to what was about to happen. Attendance, however, was poor, the guru's performance perhaps less than adequate and the movement was left in heavy financial debt. To overcome this setback, new rules were instituted to tighten up the movement. This reduced its easy appeal to many members, old and potential, especially those already disenchanted with the festival. Then in 1974 the guru married his Caucasian secretary which, due to his rule of celibacy, came as a distinct shock to many followers, with perhaps more than 50 percent of premies defecting over this issue. Somewhat corrupted by the America he had come to save, Maharaj Ji had also come by this time to affect a rather hippie style of clothing and vocabulary. He also lived in a mansion and traveled by limousine! Holy Mother had also become distressed and finally revoked his leadership. She returned to India, leaving him and his failing American membership cut off from the larger international movement. Thus, the cult remains here in very reduced form and influence, a divine light that failed!

We have very briefly examined three cults: Scientology, Hare Krsna, and the Divine Light Mission. If we recall the discussion of cult characteristics from Chapter 1, we can see many of them clearly emerge in these religions. Such traits as authority, leadership, regimentation, renunciation of the world, the search for mystical experience and ecstatic behaviors all occur in them. They do reflect a reaction to orthodox faiths as we know them in the United States. They repudiate values of the secular world. Yet, these three do differ in emphasis and in many specific details. They are clearly not identical, and the more cults one might choose to describe, the more difficult it would be to emerge with a single set of criteria with which to define them. We shall return to this difficulty in the final chapter after we have looked at more cults and at more aspects of the cult experience. We can now examine the lure of cults for prospective members.

Chapter 3

THE WHO AND WHY OF CULTS

What kind of people join cults? What motivates them to become operating thetans, to gain Krishna consciousness, or to experience God directly? The answers to such questions are not easy to come by, and data presented in scholarly and other accounts is often contradictory. There is certainly the general notion in many popular writings that the people who eventually join cults in America are not normal, that they are in some way disturbed. Yet since many cults do thrive at least for a time, surely all the members could not be of this nature. One scholar has suggested that cult members can fall into three categories. Most such people are basically "normal" and have turned to cults in a moment of need in their lives. Other people, it is suggested, have had problems or needs for considerable periods of time in their lives. These persons may deserve the label "seeker or searcher." They are looking for answers and may join a number of cults in repetitive fashion. A minority of people may be truly disturbed people. Joining a cult may permit them an avenue for the expression of such deviant tendencies. When one studies a cult as an outsider it may be difficult to separate members into such convenient categories. Which are the normal blissed-out Divine Lighters? Again, could a truly abnormal person function at all in a cult context? We can return to this question.

More specific cult studies have suggested some other answers as to what kind of people join cults. Some agreement exists as to the fact that a majority of cult members in this country have had some college background, although few may be actual graduates. Members tend to be young, in their late teens or early twenties, although some cults are exceptions to this notion. Cult members as a rule tend to be drawn from the middle class or higher classes more so than from among the disadvantaged. This, it might be added, separates cult members from those of sects whose members generally seem to be drawn from the lower classes. Cult members tend to be white in terms of "race," although this may be a by-product of class affiliation. More females seem to be attracted to cults than males, although the more successful cults may reverse this statistic! It is probably a simple truism that cult members tend to be people who did not have a heavy commitment to traditional churches since they turn to cults to answer their religious needs. Some studies do suggest that those individuals who did belong to more orthodox religious organizations were people whose previous faiths were those most accepting of their social environments; the most secularized churches produce the most likely cult candidates! It has also been remarked many times that the drug-oriented hippie counterculture of the sixties and early seventies was also a breeding ground for many converts to cults. We will presently return to this point.

While the above characters have been suggested as fairly typical of cult members, there are always specific cults whose members may not fit this model. Some of these characters may in themselves help us to understand why people join cults; others may be neutral in this respect. One always has to examine very specific studies for data to affirm or deny such statements, and often the more such studies are consulted, the more vague and less useful the characters become. A somewhat similar difficulty is encountered when we examine suggestions as to why people are motivated to join cults. Certainly the literature is large on this topic. At any rate, knowing why people join is probably more useful in understanding cults than knowing who as defined above. If we can find some agreement as to why they join we can then avoid generalities such as—people who join cults tend to be in their late teens—and substitute for that statement—people who join cults are those persons who do so for certain reasons or gain certain satisfactions from such membership. This would be more meaningful if we wish to know why cults exist!

In the examination of the why of cults I will bring together information on a number of levels to provide an overview and a sampling of motives for membership. Two general studies will be excerpted which the reader may wish to consult in detail. Full citations are provided in the bibliographic essay at the end of the chapter. We can begin with a very general study (not specifically on cults) by Philip Slater who has suggested that there are three very basic human needs that must be fulfilled in any society. American culture he believes is at present frustrating these needs. One basic need is the desire for community. We wish to live in close fellowship and cooperation with other people says Slater, but in America today, with its impersonal cities, its fragmented groups, and its drives for individual competition, such a desire is difficult to satisfy. This is probably debatable, but let's concede its truth on a very general level. Now we can ask if writers, on the whys of cults, make specific statements comparable to this. Willa Appel says "cults provide a sense of community—they are structured like a family." J. Gordon Melton and Robert L. Moore say that cults "offer the appeal of group intimacy—fellowship that satisfied a need for close contact often lacking in society." Cults give people "a place to belong." This seems pretty clearly to be what Slater is suggesting in general as a need. Cults can meet our desire for community. Remember the ashrams and premie centers, the Hare Krsna groups and Scientology orgs. These certainly operate in a family, cooperative-like atmosphere.

Slater's second major need is what he calls a desire for engagement, a need to feel we can deal directly with social problems. In today's society we do seem somewhat incapable of dealing with social issues like poverty, racism, world peace and the like. We study them, file reports, perhaps even pass a law now and then, but they do not disappear. They remain with us. Reflective people suggest they may have no standard solutions. What remarks do our cult authors make in these respects? Appel says "cult members are told that their lives have importance—they are chosen to save the world." Melton and Moore suggest along similar lines that cults "offer a remythologizing of life for converts—higher meanings and aspirations." In this way cults offer their members a non-standard, non-traditional set of mechanisms for solving social and individual problems. If we can clear the world say scientologists, how can any problems remain? Wait until everyone has Krsna consciousness and is filled with love and happiness! If we can experience God directly, we can certainly overcome social or individual problems. Such solutions derive from a different problem-solving perspective, a new way of dealing with such matters. The newness of cults makes it too soon for members to discover such solutions might fail.

Slater finally suggests that we all have a desire for dependence. We want other people to help us in guiding our lives. We want direction and yet in America today we stress independence, self-reliance, the "self-made" person; like in the song—"I did it my way." Unfortunately, all this may cause discomfort. How should we behave, what should we want, what should I be when I grow up, exactly what is my way? It's not only lonely at the top but also lonely at the bottom as well if one has to make most of one's own decisions! This certainly overstates the case as do the other needs, but let's examine cults again in this respect. Appel says, "cults give structure, purpose, routine, and order. Melton and Moore add that cults "help people get their act together with support, guidance, and discipline." Think of the daily grind in a Hare Krsna ashram. From before dawn to after dusk, all activities are planned. Not even time for non-Krsna thinking! If you want others to do your thinking for you, or much of it, if you need direction, cults can be an ideal situation. They can certainly cater to your need for dependence.

Let's examine another general study, one actually oriented towards cults and see how it matches "whys" with our more specific accounts. The theologian Harvey Cox has asked why young people in this country seem to be joining oriental cults. He has suggested five main reasons why this might be the case. First, he believes that at least initially—at the beginning of their cult careers—they are looking for simple human friendship. They want others to give them attention. This certainly matches our desire for community—cults are like a family for the reason given previously. As such, it requires no further comment. Second, he suggests young people join these cults because they see them as a special kind of experience. Converts see cults as providing a personal encounter (remember the discussion of religion in Chapter 1) with sacred/supernatural things, whereas traditional religion consists in mere "words." One could generalize from this and again hypothesize that people in the most secularized faiths or those with no traditional faith at all but with religious needs would fall into this category.

What do our experts say relative to this reason for cult membership? Appel says that cults are believed to give their members access to special power. Members feel that "God" is paying special attention to them. They feel different and special. Melton and Moore believe that in these "non-conventional" religions there is a kind of real spiritual immediacy, a personal contact with a reality beyond ourselves not found in mainline faiths. They suggest that this reality need not necessarily be God in the usual sense. Consider our cult examples. Scientology allows us to reach the thetan-being within us. Divine Light allows us to directly experience "God." Activities in the Hare Krsna bring us closer to Krsna and closer still after death. What more immediacy can one ask? What orthodox western faith challenges the believer in such a fashion?

Cox also mentions that people turn to Eastern oriental cults because they are looking for authority. Confronted specifically with "choice fatigue" in modern society they want to be given answers—simple answers that make sense so they can alleviate confusion. People desire a road to follow constructed by persons they can look up to, as possessing greater truths. This motive too we have seen before. It is Slater's desire for dependence. Cox adds fourthly that cults seem more "natural" to those who join them. They reveal a sense of unspoiled purity and simplicity. They represent a kind of counter to modern technological civilization. In doing so they cater to our discontent with the things of Western civilization, being in essence, I suppose, a kind of Eastern mystery versus Western fact kind of alternative! It is a bit more difficult to find precise equivalents in statements from our experts in this respect. However, Appel does mention that joining a cult may often be prompted by and seen as a form of rebellion. It can be a rejection both of parents and of the cultural status quo. Melton and Moore, looking at it more positively, see joining cults as a way of asserting adulthood and independence. I suppose if the avenue taken here is different from the ordinary, then the ensuing contrast makes everything so much the better!

The simple yet busy life-styles of the members of most cults seem to reflect the above statements. One can add to this the various prohibitions or taboos one encounters within them in terms of food, drugs, alcohol, tobacco, sex, and the like. These are intended to ensure purity and, not incidentally, to pose a counter to the outside world which is thereby not only rendered different but rejected. In some respects, Cox's last reason fits close to this way of thinking. He believes that people join these cults, to a much lesser extent than the other reasons, because of health concerns. Health and purity certainly are often thought of as aspects of the same thing, with life-style playing a key role in attaining either of them. Some cults do provide health-enhancing techniques: for example, being audited in Scientology clears away all problems and allows one to function in a superhuman sort of way. Many Caribbean and other cults we shall examine in the second part of this book also deal with illness in a very specific and directed fashion. Appel and Melton and Moore do not comment directly on such motives.

We have examined Slater and Cox and have seen their suggestions as to why people join cults are nicely reinforced by even more specific comments by other writers. Some other scholars have attempted to reduce all reasons along these lines into a single framework and state this in terms of a uniting general hypothesis. We may briefly note one such example. The sociologists Charles Glock and Rodney Stark see the ultimate secret in the appeal of such groups to be found in relative deprivation. This is, in their definition, any and all of the ways that an individual or group may be or feel disadvantages in comparison either to other individuals or groups or to an internalized set of standards. In other words, I will possibly join a cult if I feel I am less well off in some way that I think I should be or if I feel this way when I compare myself to others. Since groups of people may feel this way also, cults may be actively generated by relative deprivation.

The desire for family, authority, to solve problems, and find purpose and health, in short all the reasons we have previously discussed, certainly find a home under this concept of relative deprivation. This may be all the more so if I feel deprived based upon my own standards rather than in comparison to others. These writers neatly encapsulate our thinking and perhaps add to it when they delineate five basic types of relative deprivation: economic, social, organismic, ethical and psychic. In order, these suggest the following: limited access to necessities or luxuries in life; less prestige, power, status, or opportunities for social participation; lack of good mental or physical health; value conflicts between one's values and those of society; or no meaningful system of values at all—the "little lost sheep" syndrome! I believe our earlier discussion has suggested all of these, but this scheme does summarize things in a neat way. We can now turn to more descriptively based studies.

A great many specific studies deal with why people join a particular cult. These generally reinforce our list of broad reasons why a person might seek membership in such groups. Such studies sometimes also bring up more particularistic causes. We can examine three cases in point as representative, saving others for the next chapter on the dynamics of the conversion experience. That data overlaps with the present chapter. As a first case in point we can consider a cult we have already gained familiarity with: the Divine Light Mission. James Downton, Jr. has studied the phases of conversion to this group and in the process has elicited background information giving testimony, among other things, to some of the "whys" of cult membership.

Downton's findings reveal that at least half of this sample of converts had experienced family difficulties. The ideals of their parents and family expectations created frustration and guilt in these young people who felt their sense of autonomy to be hindered in its expression. They were, in the sense previously described, rebellious and their family situations also included other difficulties such as parents who were constantly fighting or who were divorced. Compounding family problems for these people was the difficulty that they appear to have no really developed spiritual outlook. Many had left their parents' churches in adolescence, seeing conventional religion in critical terms; like they saw their parents! So, mainline religion was not available for support in their situation. These were not uneducated young persons. Remember Chapter 2. Most reported that they had experienced early schooling in rather positive terms, especially its social side. By high school and college, however, they had not developed any really clear sense of what they wished to do with their lives. Here is our deprivation of meaning, our need for direction. Some of these had also become socially alienated as well, having considerable difficulty in relating to their peers as well as to their family.

At this point these prospective Divine Light Mission members began to drop out into the 1960s "counterculture" and experiment with psychedelic drugs. Downton points out that they were generally led to do so by an acquaintance or relative, a point we consider later in Chapter 4. Clearly, they saw their experience with drugs as opening up a new awareness and a desire to have such experiences in normal consciousness. In other words, they wished to feel special and different all of the time. At the same time, the drug experiences tended to further undermine their already weak or non-existent Western concept of a personal god. Visionary events with drugs gave them a more Eastern concept of "a force holding the cosmos together," a conceptualization not unlike that of Divine Light theology.

Many drug culture experiences were short, not lasting, and some were terrifying bad trips. The people in Downton's sample were searching for an alternative and as this cult began to spread it provided just such an alternative. They heard of it from premies and others already in the movement and were especially attracted by the claim that through the knowledge sessions they could get a direct experience of God. Remember that such experiences were "blissed out" events somewhat like the earlier drug experiences. In fact, two thirds of the sample of people in this study were immediately ecstatic and many who were not did eventually have that experience. The experience itself along with reinforcement from others in the movement was followed by at least a short period of great enthusiasm. The converts believed their lives had taken a turn for the better; they knew the truth, they were with likeminded others in a family situation. The cult met many of the needs of these people in a legal way that the drug subculture did not!

The drug experience may have had an as yet not completely recognized catalyzing role in cult membership growth in the 1960s. A second specific series of studies on a cult demonstrates this very clearly as well as providing additional information and insight. These concern the Meher Baba cult studied by Thomas Robbins and others. Meher Baba, "compassionate father," is a now deceased guru from India. He was born in Poona in 1894 and had supernatural experiences as a youth, ultimately claiming to be a manifestation of God on earth (avatar). He eventually established a spiritual center near Myrtle Beach, South Carolina, and attracted many drug-centered individuals due to his claim that drugs were physically dangerous and spiritually futile, claiming that himself was "the highest of the high." This message attracted persons interested in "highs." There may be as many as seven thousand members today, but their general lack of street recruiting has given this cult low visibility and so it is less known to the public than some of the others discussed in this book. Most members form small local groups around persons more charismatic than themselves and meet to talk and to relate positive experiences in their lives.

The basic message is somewhat de-emphasized in this cult, since Meher Baba was not truly concerned with formal principles. He said "I have not come to teach but to awaken." There is, however, the notion that all people are one; they have a meta-physical unity of which he is the personification. He is the universal soul which is the higher self of every individual! As the "Divine Beloved," he is the source of all love and love is the mechanism through which we can sense our oneness with others. The highest love is divine love in which a person (the lover) has no being apart from the beloved. If intense enough, one can thus gain union with God. Therefore, followers see their relationship to this guru as very personal. He also was felt to manipulate the experiences of members; confronting them with challenges, getting them jobs, and providing other opportunities. As he is part of everyone in the unity of all people, we can see him in ourselves and in others. A favorite phrase of members is "I see Baba in you" as a sign of spiritual progress.

Spiritual advancement in this cult involves the integration of action and detachment. When a member acts in the world—works at a job or whatever—he or she dedicates their activity to Baba and does not do it for the earthly rewards of such activity. This generates an attitude of "in but not of the world," a freedom from ego involvement. The consequences, so to speak, are in the master's hands. In this sense, Robbins sees this cult as serving as a kind of halfway house for bringing drug culture dropouts back into society. The cult mystical experience is substituted for the drug experience with the same expansion of consciousness and knowledge. Drugs and mysticism are replaced by Baba and mysticism and, then, armed with new knowledge that Baba regulates one's life, Baba and worldly involvement. Members can drop back into conventional society armed with a new perspective and backed by a new support group.

Robbins and another scholar have also suggested, based on a study of the members of this cult, why these people initially became members of the counterculture. In their view modern society oppresses youth (remember Slater) because they have to go from very personal, primary family relations to very impersonal ones as they become older. In this setting of alienation they become "love starved" as well as needing ultimate answers. In their drug culture days, the drugs may have expanded consciousness but they dominated life and interfered with any solution to the problem of love. The Baba cult, in its local support groups and especially at the center near Myrtle Beach, is seen to overcome that difficulty. The cult provides answers but also supplies the necessary social qualities to life. The interaction among the members is "personal, familial, and intimate" with hugs, kisses, and smiles to heighten a sense of belonging. The center is an expressive community like the Hare Krsna and Divine Light groups.

Not all cults, of course, mainly attract ex-drug users or counterculture types. Many attract what was earlier called the seeker-searcher type of person. This is the case even if the message of the cult seems a bit more bizarre than usual. A last specific example can be used to illustrate this point. The case in point is called the Bo and Peep cult after nicknames for its founders and has been reported on by Robert Balch and David Taylor. The founders of this cult are a former music teacher and a nurse who met each other in 1972 and became convinced that they had a "higher purpose." Ultimately, they claimed to be members of the Kingdom of Heaven who had taken human bodies to help us overcome our purely human level of existence. Their message is as follows. All forms of life evolve slowly but steadily to a higher level of consciousness. In a sense of apparent reincarnation they advance through a succession of lifetimes and move to higher grades. If we as humans can abandon our past here on earth—one of many gardens in the universe that support life—we can make a connection to the next highest level and reach a point where we can convert into an androgenous being. This is accomplished by chemical changes, "human individual metamorphosis," and will leave a person with an indestructible body. If one can also overcome all human emotions and worldy attachment, which keep us on the purely human level, then we will be taken to Heaven in a flying saucer! To aid in these processes one must leave family and friends, give up your job, and travel around the country with a small group of like-minded persons. Living a spartan existence and camping out, one is assigned a partner, usually of the opposite sex, with whom one develops "friction." This aids in gaining awareness of the human qualities that must be overcome.

Rather amazingly to most of us (I would guess) within seven months of holding their first meeting, Bo and Peep (the shepherds) may have attracted well over one hundred followers. Most as we might expect were in their early twenties, but some were as old as fifty-eight. While some had college education, most had less education and generally had held a succession of low status employments. The recruitment of these people seems to have been instantaneous. They would be attracted to a brief lecture noted in health food store advertisements and other places. They became interested and returned the next day for a more informal discussion and in two days would be taken to or directed to a "buffer camp" where they were absorbed into the cult. All of this occurred without most of the conversion stages discussed in the next chapter! They then practiced the friction technique and meditation as the groups moved about the countryside in response to the directions of the leaders who were not always present. Bo and Peep did promise to be on hand before the flying saucer arrived.

What was the appeal of this cult? In Balch and Taylor's understanding the prospective members were already "metaphysical seekers." They evidenced (from interviews) an intense desire for the truth. Most had explored many other teachings and had already lost much of their commitment to conventional society and its answers. Realizing that there are "many paths to the top of the mountain" they were already in a cultic milieu as seeker-searchers and there was a new and certainly different style of message to explore. Bo and Peep's version of the truth offered an escape from the planet Earth! Even when the cult went secret in 1976 and had lost members, the dropouts insisted that while they had come to reject the message of this cult its leaders had aided their spiritual growth if only by hastening their rejection of secular, mundane attachments.

The bottom line here seems to be that if you are into personal growth in the setting of the cultic milieu, it becomes a try, try again routine without any long process of joining or any specific "why" being involved. Cult membership becomes opportunistic on the part of the seeker! Surely at some level this may operate for many converts to cults.

We have examined a number of reasons for joining cults and we will return to this question in the final chapter of this book. Clearly, there are some general as well as specific needs met through cult membership. There are also catalysts prompting a move to solve needs in a specific cult or in the metaphysical frameworks cults have to offer. Can these things be brought together? Does a model, even incomplete, exist that can help us gain a feel for the overall process? The answer is yes, in a limited sense. We explore this notion in the following chapter.

Chapter 4

THE PROCESS OF CONVERSION

People join cults for a variety of reasons. How do they actually join? What is the process of conversion? Does the "why" and "how" fit together? As mentioned in the previous chapter, several schemes do exist suggesting how all such behaviors fit into a kind of master framework. While a complete schema does not as yet exist, in fact given the diversity of cult types it may never exist, some models have been suggested. Certainly insightful comments that fall short of actual models also occur. In this present chapter we can examine a few of these to build on what has been previously discussed.

Willa Appel has neatly summarized the process of conversion. Cults must, she says, somehow attract the attention of a potential convert. They must isolate such a person from his or her past life (if this has not already happened). Then they must "destroy" that person's old personality; cause changes in their intellectual and emotional commitment to their past life. This causes the convert to then assume a new world view and a new identity as the cult member. Remember the new activities, dress, taboos, and other aspects described for the Hare Krsna cult!

John Lofland and Rodney Stark have, however, taken this basic process and devised a rather elegant model for the entire cult-joining process. In their model they suggest that two sets of conditions or factors are involved in conversion. First, there are certain predisposing conditions. These are background factors; things relative to a person before he or she has any contact with a specific cult. These conditions partially include our list of needs from Chapter 3. Second are the situational factors. These arise from the interaction between the cult members and a potential convert. Both conditions are critical for conversion to take place. Within this context Lofland and Stark delineate seven basic phases. Each phase leads to the next, although some may be fairly simultaneous for some persons.

The first phase is that of tension. This state of affairs can be the result of the needs previously discussed; needs for friendship, direction, and the like, or from deprivations in Glock's terms; psychic or whatever. The point is that in this phase the potential convert feels such problems to be very real and that his or her affairs are far from ideal. It is suggested that such an individual also feels or experiences this state of tension over long periods of time. The second phase involves the type of problem-solving perspective chosen by the potential convert. Certainly, any number of ways exist to deal with long-term tension: psychiatric, political, perhaps even a program of jogging or physical fitness. It is suggested however that potential cult converts seem exceptionally uninformed about such conventional tension-reducing means for relief and, very importantly, for gaining a definition of their problems. What these people do share in common is a general propensity for imposing religious meanings on their difficulties.

The next phase is seekership. Based on the above, the potential converts come to define themselves as religious seekers/searchers. They may shift from church to church, but, given the usual non-religious or non-orthodox aspects commented upon previously, it is more often the cultic milieu that attracts their attention. Whatever the format, it is suggested by these authors that the overarching idea is that the supernatural can intervene in the secular world (remember Meher Baba) and that such a possibility may permit a resolution of the tension situation.

The three phases discussed so far are predisposing conditions. Now those of the situational nature come into play. Phase four is the turning point. This occurs either slightly before or about the time of meeting cult members. In either case, in this phase the potential convert reaches what is perceived as a turning point in his or her life. This may be due to flunking out of college, losing a job, moving from one area of the country to another, or whatever. Such persons are faced with a need to do something different, and this turning-point event increases their awareness of this situation and at the same time gives them the opportunity to do so! Their commitment to much of their past lives and behaviors has diminished. New possibilities present themselves. A person is free from past and older obligations.

The next phase of the conversion model is that of cult affective bonds. These refer to the influence on the convert from individuals already within the cult. If a person is to be drawn into a cult, some emotional/affective ties must develop if they do not already pre-exist. Importantly, these ties may develop even before one has come to know the specific teachings of the cult or has accepted them. When the potential convert accepts the members, other aspects of cult involvement may follow. If this part of the model is an adequate description of reality, it does imply how important and primary the friendship-family aspects of cult membership may be. Clearly, if a void exists prior to the cult situation, if a relative or friend has already found the "truth" of the cult, movement through this stage is apt to progress more quickly. But even bonds unsupported by any previous connection may build quickly. Such are often depicted as almost instantaneous! "I knew as soon as I saw him/her that they were gifted with the truth and were happy—I liked them immediately and wanted to be like them." The charisma of the leaders and earnestness and conviction of followers no doubt go a long way in promoting such immediate reactions. Recall how quickly Bo and Peep were able to convince their followers!

The next phase, often simultaneous and opposed to the above, is that of extra-cult affective bonds. This represents the counter-emotional influences of family and friends who attempt to influence the individual not to join the cult. If a person has left all previous social attachments behind, if they are "social atoms," then this is not a phase. Likewise, for many converts who do have outside attachments this may also hardly create difficulties because such relatives and friends may not be aware of what is happening. They may only become aware of the person's commitment to the cult after the fact. Again, the degree of need for friendship correlates here, suggesting social ties not being too intact. At any rate, when outsiders are aware of a person being drawn into a cult and if they are against this, conversion is made more difficult. Often, a great deal of emotional warfare occurs at this point; a tug of war over the person by those within and without the cult. The responses of families and others is so obviously crucial that we will return to it as a separate topic later in this chapter.

Finally, if the insiders win the battle for the soul of the convert, or face no opposition, the last phase, intensive interaction, occurs. In order to become a complete cult member rather than simply a "verbal convert," intensive interaction with cult members is necessary. Here, in isolation, cut off from the outside, the message of the cult and deep feelings of belonging to it can be inculcated into the new member. This is the arena of the ashram, the local Scientology org, the headquarters of the Meher Baba followers, and it is in this context that the full impact of the cult hits the convert. It is in this situation that what some critics of cults call brainwashing occurs. We return to this concept presently. Before looking at suggestions on aspects of conversion supplied by other authors we can examine the specifics of these later phases in more detail with respect to the techniques of one specific cult, the Moonies.

No American cult seems to arouse so many strong emotions as the Moonies, so it is inevitable that at some point we bring them into this book. The Moonies, named after their leader Sun Myung Moon, is really the Unification Church; the American branch of the Holy Spirit Association for the Unification of World Christianity. This title is equivalent to the Hare Krsna Iskon contrast discussed previously. The present organization is a movement intended to unify all world religions and create a world family to usher in the kingdom of God on earth. It was founded by the South Korean evangelist Moon, who believed that Jesus appeared to him when he was a youth and instructed Moon to complete Jesus' mission begun many hundreds of years earlier. He apparently began to preach around 1945 and after imprisonment in North Korea really began to organize his present group in 1958 based on writings called the Divine Principle. In 1959 the cult sent a missionary to California and Moon himself arrived there in 1972 to arouse the American branch of the organization to greater activity. This was successful and resulted in the recruitment of several thousand new members, often by high-pressure techniques we will describe shortly.

In simplest terms, Moon's message is as follows. All the problems of human history go back to the Garden of Eden. Adam and Eve failed to follow God's commands and form a family without sin as a model for succeeding generations. We should have God as the family head, male and female as coequal, and children at the bottom as the basis for relations, but the primal failure not only derailed this but in addition Lucifer has taken God's place. Through seduction of Eve he has become the spiritual parent of humankind. Hence, our fall from grace and our being cut off from God. To alleviate our present problems we must reverse all of this. God and the proper family must re-emerge, and quickly, since we are living in the last days. In this respect, communism represents the culmination of Satan's world. We must live centered on God, and the Unification Church can bring us together properly as "true parents"—people who have had our original sin removed and who can now live centered on God as we were meant to be originally. All this is with Moon as the messenger of God. To aid in this task Christ will come again in Korea as a man in the flesh. It should be mentioned that Moon's followers are divided as to whether he is that messiah, and he himself is vague concerning that suggestion. At any rate, when we are all united by building a world family by uniting all religions with Christianity as central, a kingdom of God will be established here on earth, perhaps by the year 2001. At that point we shall all live in brotherly love with God as our parent. This is a very simplistic and incomplete sense of the ideas of this cult.

John Lofland has studied how recruitment to the Moonies took place in California. Due to the somewhat loose organization of this cult different techniques occur elsewhere. This author suggests the following five sequential mechanisms for bringing in new converts. These correspond to the latter phases of the model previously discussed. First is picking up. Members make casual contact with prospective members in a public place such as a train or bus station. They look for persons who look "new in town" and who may be lonely and invite them to a dinner and lecture at a nearby house. The cult members are well scrubbed and enthusiastic and they mute or deny any religious aspects. The invitation seems innocuous enough, especially if some young person is seeking friendship. Second comes hooking. The invitee arrives at the designated location to find a number of young people, some persons much like himself, and is assigned a "buddy" who remains at his side. This person learns as much about the background of the potential convert as possible so that conversation can later be directed in a sympathetic fashion—"Yes, some of us are college dropouts, too." This is learning what kind of hooks other people can follow up on to pull the person deeper into the group. A meal is followed by a rather entertaining lecture on principles that bind the group together—sharing, loving, working for the good of humankind. These can hardly be considered controversial and no mention is made of the Moonies. An invitation is extended to a fun weekend on a nearby farm.

If the prospect agrees, he or she is then effectively isolated and intensive interaction with cult members follows, what Lofland calls encapsulating. All waking moments are planned to completely absorb the attention of the guests and one's buddy is always present. All activities focus attention on the group and many of these, games, weeding crops, etc., are very fatigue-inducing. This, along with minimal food and few rest periods, produces a lowering of mental awareness. Of course, the input is strictly limited, as topics appropriate to the group dominate conversation. Finally, Moonie ideology is slowly but systematically presented, from very basic to bland assertions to more controversial concepts. As this is done "love bombing" occurs. The prospect is literally drenched with love and approval and this is enough to make anyone, especially one needing affection, find it difficult to reject the doctrine that accompanies that love. Any reservations or counter thoughts are clearly seen as cutting off that level! Hesitation is drowned in calls to loving solidarity. "Don't you like us?" At the end of the weekend the most likely prospects are invited to stay for a weeklong workship and then even longer. As the target remains longer and is gradually drawn in deeper and accepts Unification Church ideology, his or her doubts are then interpreted as the influence of Lucifer. In Appel's terms, a new intellectual orientation has occurred. This Lofland calls committing. It now becomes more and more difficult to return to one's past world. One can see in this specific example how the later stages of the conversion model can specifically work.

Other writers have commented on the nature of conversion and its techniques and we can turn briefly to two such accounts, both for repetition of what has been said above and for additional insights. Luther Gerlach and Virginia Hine in their book on social movements have suggested that commitment is the key to joining any organization of the type we have been discussing. They recognize seven steps to the commitment process. Their steps broadly overlap what has already been considered as well as suggesting several new notions on which to focus attention. First, the group (cult, in our case) must make initial contact with a prospective member. This equates to picking up, in Lofland's terminology. Second, the cult members must refocus the needs of the potential convert. This is to say they must redefine his or her discontents, deprivations, or whatever in terms of the ideology of their group. "We are the family you have been looking for; we are raising the consciousness of the whole world to save it." Gerlach and Hine suggest an important technique here is by demonstrations by present members as to how their lives have been changed for the better. "I was once lost like you, but now things are great." This is very close to the hooking previously described. There is nothing more alluring than to see oneself in the mirror of possibility. "If they made it with the help of this group, maybe I can too!"

A third step in the commitment process is re-education through group interaction. Ties are built to present group members. This is equivalent to the intensive interaction of Lofland. It also involves building up new ideas and expectations in the mind of the convert and the notion that only the group can secure these things. Fourth is decision and surrender.

The convert gives up his or her old identity and also gives control for themselves over to the group leaders and other members. This may, of course, involve changes in physical identity such as new styles of clothing, manners of speech, hours for activity, and the like. Remember changes in Hare Krsna members! Next comes the commitment event itself. The convert undergoes an emotional change and a realization of freedom, cosmic wholeness, salvation or purpose; in short, a sense that finally his or her needs are being met. This act seals the identity changes previously undergone and functions as well as a kind of bridge-burning act! Going back to regular behaviors and society becomes very difficult from this point on.

I would suggest that the above constitutes a kind of second turning point. As has been suggested previously, the first involves something that frees a person to explore the world of cults to obtain need satisfaction; the second comes in total commitment when that need satisfaction has been developed. To reinforce these changes and make them a reality for the individual, Gerlach and Hine suggest that step six is to have the convert testify on his or her new condition. As they tell others—including prospective new members—how life has changed for the better, this makes such changes all the more real and valuable to that person and to themselves. Ultimately, in the last step of the commitment process the group reinforces the convert's changed ways of thinking and behaving, giving them as it were the final stamp of approval. It should be understood, of course, that these latter steps may be almost simultaneous.

A slightly different way of looking at this general topic comes from the work of Rosabeth Kanter in a general book on commitment. She sees commitment to any organization of these sorts (utopian in nature) as involving six processes. These processes can help us focus on everything that has been said previously along these lines. The specific relevance is the notion that if these do not occur, membership may be short-lived despite a person's needs or may not even occur. These processes probably work more or less together in a cult in terms of time, although some could proceed and stimulate others. One supposes this would differ from different converts. At any rate, these six processes build up and ensure the commitment of individuals to the group.

One process is sacrifice. If a person has to give up something of value to belong to a group, be it drugs, alcohol, meat, an affluent life-style or whatever, they can gain a kind of vested interest in continuing membership in that group. "I didn't give up these things for nothing." Not only does sacrifice create commitment, but it may become a kind of "psychic cross" to bear in the process. Second, and clearly related to points made previously, is investment. Here, Kanter refers to the process of gaining a stake in the group in terms of time and energy. One comes to make a non-returnable investment of these things in the cult. To leave is to negate that investment and this may be of a financial nature as well. Having done so much and then to leave would be wasteful as long as some satisfactions exist.

Both sacrifice and investment are closely related as processes. They are also perhaps close to a third process Kanter calls renunciation. Here, what is given up is something social: the giving up of relations with people outside the cult. This may include family, friends, and secular world contacts and activities. Exclusive contacts are to cult members. This is the cult affective bonds of Lofland and Stark. Here it is not just that one must have left people behind for a reason—an investment that must pay off—but the ties so created to cult members may make it difficult to again resume normal social relations. Of course, one may have joined the cult seeking the friendship we have spoken of before, and process number four, communion, can be important for some individuals. Communion means bringing members into contact with the group in such a way that they feel a oneness with it and develop a "we" feeling. Kanter suggests this is helped by communal sharing and work, regular group contact, and rituals. Think back again to the ashrams and to other communal elements of the Bo and Peep cult, the Hare Krsnas, and the followers of Meher Baba.

A fifth process is mortification. In becoming a cult member, one is really exchanging his or her old social and psychic identity for that of the cult. The more the procedures of these groups strip away that old identity, the more the individual has to become committed to that group. If one accepts, for example, that Baba works through you, causes events in your life to occur, the more necessary it becomes to have others "see" Baba in you! This means one has to cling more to the cult for satisfaction. Lastly, there is the process of transcendence. Kanter sees this as the process whereby an individual attaches his decision-making prerogative to a power greater than himself. In our cult context this means submitting to the leaders and others in the cult for often minute guidance in all aspects of behavior. If one is looking for authority to begin with, the commitment-enhancing aspects of this process are obvious. Even if some other need is the basis of affiliation to the cult, the charisma of leaders, the comprehensive ideology that is "soaked up" in the cult context can draw one in deeper and deeper. It is this aspect perhaps more than the others which has led to accusations of brainwashing by critics of cults. We shortly return to this point. Clearly, there are powerful forces working here to secure the commitment of members to cults and other groups. If we put the views of Kanter, Gerlach and Hine, and Lofland together, we can see an obvious overlap in viewing how a person comes to join a cult in process terms. This despite the fact they are all taking a slightly different perspective on this topic. One wonders how a person can ever come to leave a cult. How can a person drop out with such lures at work? Having discussed getting in we can now look at getting out.

Except for the literature on deprogramming, one senses that less attention has been paid to the process of leaving cults than as to how one comes to join them. This issue can be combined with general reactions to cults since pressure, parental or otherwise, often helps to determine the effectiveness of membership in cults. Remember the phase of extra-cult affective bonds! It is clear that members do leave cults both due to outside pressure and on their own accord. Appel says that about one third of members eventually leave, although specific studies vary by cult in this respect. Also, the longer one has been a member, the more difficult it may be to extricate oneself or be removed from the cult. Here, Kanter's processes have had a longer time to work.

Reasons for leaving may vary. As implied above, if a person has continued to maintain valid attachments to family and friends external to the cult, then their influence may eventually come to prevail. Then, too, a person may become disillusioned as in the Divine Light Mission case; what the cult promises and what it actually delivers may turn off members who may eventually become tired of the demands of membership itself. The needs impelling members to originally join may also not be satisfied. Then they will return to the secular world or join still another cult along the lines of the seeker/searcher model discussed previously. Members may even grow out of the values a cult has to offer as they grow older. Many of the needs we highlighted in an earlier chapter are peculiarly sensitive for youth! We can add to these reasons for leaving cults the more sensationalist kidnap/rescue and deprogramming activities. These were particularly common a decade or so ago and involve parents and others forcibly removing the person from the cult. To gain a sense of this we have to briefly note the overall responses to cults.

Three general levels of responses to cults have occurred: family, religious and political. That essentially negative responses have occurred at all should come as no surprise. Whenever new faiths have begun in the past they generally have provoked negativism from previous faiths and power structures. Cults challenge the status quo as well as the legitimacy or exclusiveness of previously existing groups. Quite often these groups respond in "knee jerk" fashion branding the new faith as heretical, evil, exploitative, or whatever. In our present context, perhaps the first of the above to suggest that cults posed a threat were Christian evangelical leaders and fellow religious travelers. In fact, several denominations eventually established counter-cult organizations to actively impede the success of cults. While such groups do not often agree on the exact nature of the cults they are opposed to, finding them as difficult to define as the scholars in Chapter 1, they do see them as contradicting orthodox Christian beliefs and practices. On a deeper level, they also appear to see cults as creations of Satan. Certainly these views were enhanced by the drop in church membership and influence in the sixties and seventies in the United States. Many members were lost to these cults and "good" religions don't compete for members! These churches have perhaps devoted most of their time to informing present members of their congregations as to the evil and heresy of cults, but some attempts have also been made to take the war to the enemy, to distribute literature to cult members as to the evils of their specific cults and to suggest a return to orthodoxy for salvation.

The response of government has been more equivocal in these respects. Politicians and others have apparently been less quick to see cults as a threat to political interests, although historically this is less true. The occasional cult tragedy such as the Jonestown suicides has galvanized some activity, but most has been reactive. Parents of cult members have often attempted to influence legislation. They have provoked legislators to sponsor bills giving parents conservatory rights over their children (as in the case of a patient no longer rational enough to make their own decisions). Proposed bills have also required full disclosure of cult teachings and related matters. Legislative bodies and the courts have however been reluctant to interfere with what they seem to regard as private family matters. The issue of religious freedom also intrudes at this level. So, aside from the occasional income tax case (Sun Myung Moon recently served a jail term over this) and pressures against cults that interfere too much with local politics (the Rajneesh Foundation International on the

West Coast), and in a few other situations, the influence on cults from the political sphere has been rather muted.

This is not the case at the family level. Here, of course, one encounters cults most closely due to members actually being in the cults. As such, families are more willing to take action against what they see as a direct threat to their own existence. Many parents of cult members have not only responded locally but have joined national organizations such as the Citizens Freedom Foundation, which had 1500 members in 1975. It is groups like these that attempt to engage political process in their fight against cults, historically directing attention towards specific cults; at first, the Children of God and later the Moonies! Their major successes have been rather specific in scope however and involve deprogramming as developed by Ted Patrick and others in the early 1970s. This technique has been so controversial that courts have taken up issues of civil liberties with respect to it and the National Council of Churches has gone on record as opposing it as unchristian.

What is involved here? Simply put, because there are many usages of the word, deprogramming assumes that cult members have been brainwashed. They can no longer think for themselves and are being manipulated by cult leaders. Therefore, lacking free will of their own they must be removed from the cult context (by force and deception if necessary) and restored to "normal" by another process of brainwashing; looked at positively in this case. Through deprogramming they can be free from the evil influences of the cult. How does this work? Melton and Moore have given an excellent picture of the process of deprogramming. Parents and deprogramming "experts" find a way to temporarily isolate the cult member ("zombie") from the cult. They then kidnap him or her and take them to a house unknown to cult members who might attempt rescue. There they apply seven pressures to restore that person to proper ways of thought and behavior.

The first of these pressures is environmental control: the confinement of the cult member in a room. Next, someone, often a former cult member previously deprogrammed, stays with the deprogramee twenty-four hours a day. Thus, there is no sense of privacy. Such behaviors remind one of the exclusive input some Moonies use on their previously described country weekends! Adding to this thought is the practice of severely limiting time for sleep. Long deprogramming sessions occur and then the exhausted target is given just a little rest and then is rudely reawakened for more of the same. Fourthly, there is personal abuse.

Sometimes this is physical—shaking, being tied up—but mostly this takes psychological forms. These include verbal abuse, being told how one was misled, was foolish, and the like, how one hurt one's parents, and they intended to create guilt in the subject over what he or she has done. Parents and other family members beg, cry, and generally reinforce what deprogrammers are saying and doing. This is an additional pressure.

A sixth pressure is what Melton and Moore call the invasion of sacred space. Deprogrammers and others present denounce and ridicule the most sacred aspects of the cult in question. They present counter-arguments to its doctrine, ridicule its behaviors, they force the subject to eat food that is considered taboo or engage in behaviors forbidden by the cult, and tear up pictures of the leaders or founder. This is to shock the participant into new awareness. Finally, there is continual interrogation. This is a dialogue, sometimes a monologue, that accompanies all the other pressures. Questions, comments, arguments over the heretical/evil nature of the cult doctrine and activity is unrelenting. Presumably, this aids in re-establishing normal, critical thinking in the mind of the cult member. The total effect, however, is to cause physical, mental, and emotional fatigue along with humiliation and guilt in the subject who also becomes aware of the implied notion that the way out of this very uncomfortable situation is to be "normal." It should be observed here that it would be difficult for a person of the most orthodox faith to defend it under circumstances such as these!

Even for cult members who "snap out" of their errors, as it is called by some deprogrammers, the process is not over after the subject says they are sorry that they joined the cult. There follows a period during which such people are said to "float," remembering their past experiences in the cult, its values and attractions, and often thinking of returning to it. In light of this they are never left alone without support people to divert their attention. In fact, during this time and later, they may be forced to participate in the deprogramming of other persons so they can see how brainwashed they themselves had been. A full process of recovery usually takes more than one year. It has often been observed in light of all of this that deprogramming may be bad or worse than the cult membership! It certainly does employ many cult techniques. The procedure has declined in the 1980s. Aside from the legal aspects not discussed in this book there are a number of related issues here.

We can ask first of all if deprogramming works. The answer is an equivocable yes and no. Some people do snap back to what they were like before encountering the cult. Others, however, escape again and again to the cult milieu; this despite repeated deprogrammings. Which response occurs may partly be due to future need satisfactions outside the cult, and in fact parental involvement in the process may bring some families closer together and may overcome the former need for friendship. Along these lines, a question must be asked relative to the assumption of the brainwashing the process seeks to overcome. As was suggested previously, if some people leave cults voluntarily, could they have been brainwashed? If part of deprogramming is to argue with and engage in a dialogue with the subject, was that person brainwashed or was some reason left? Many scholars feel brainwashing by cults to be a myth perpetuated by families and some ex-members of cults. Families, finding it difficult to explain why their sons and daughters would leave them and give allegiance to cult leaders, can escape a sense of their own failure and guilt by saying that their children were brainwashed into leaving through no fault of the family. The kids couldn't help themselves.

The ex-members can also get off the hook as it were by claiming brainwashing. If deprogramming shows them how silly and naive they were to join the cult, they can say that they were not really responsible for their actions, that they had in fact been brainwashed. Accounts by deprogrammed "apostates" as to how they were brainwashed by one or another cult have been seized upon by anti-cultists as the basis for many of their activities! Such accounts and family interpretations, however, do not constitute evidence that brainwashing ever occurred. The participation of deprogrammed members in similar sessions and in writing anti-cult accounts of their "captivity" is in marked contrast to the generally non-involved feelings of former cult members who simply drop out of their cults. Brainwashing is probably more a rationale than a fact in most cases.

It should also be remarked that families are not monolithic in their attitudes towards cults. Their views differ as much as those of former cult members. James Beckford has made some interesting studies in England of families with children in the Unification Church. In his view family responses differ in many respects and as to why their children joined them. He sees three somewhat differing cases. One family response is that of incomprehension. This response, by only a few families in his sample, involved an inability of the family to make any sense out of their member having joined the cult. They had no idea why a son or daughter would become a Moonie! In fact, this carried over to much of what their child had done in the past. Parents confessed that they really did not know what to expect next. Their uncertainty here is a general frustration with the child and not antagonism towards the cult as such. They were resigned to the fact of membership and did not feel motivated to attempt any interference with that state of affairs or even learn anything about the cult. Beckford concluded that the social relations in these families were perhaps lacking in warmth to begin with and that the cult members had already been seekers, the current involvement with the Moonies merely representing their most recent "transformation."

The second and most frequent family response was anger; expectable in light of what we have previously discussed. These parents tried to learn all they could about the cult and it is here that the notion was common that their kids had been brainwashed. Their anger included deprogramming attempts as practical as well as legitimate means of intervening in the situation. Beckford felt that these parents, while strict, had nevertheless developed strong and affectionate family ties with their children. Hence the anger when a son or daughter joined the Moonies and the "reasonableness" of the brainwashing explanation. What else could explain such behavior! Again, this makes sense in terms of what we have said before.

The final response was one of ambivalence. Parents in this grouping did express concern over a child joining the cult but also saw it as part of a "growth experience" on the part of that person. In fact, parents in these families appear to have encouraged their children to be independent; were less strict authority figures and were now caught between what they had encouraged and what they believed to be an experiment in the wrong direction. As a result, they were anxious and did attempt to learn something about the cult. They were, however, not driven to actively interfere with that membership and did not consider brainwashing to be involved. They did not associate membership with a rejection of themselves! Beckford's study is an indication that we need to do much more research from the family end if we wish to understand the full range of extra cult responses and influences and perhaps uncover, in the process, motives influencing cult membership. Having briefly and very incompletely surveyed some aspects of the career of cult members—getting in and getting out—we can now turn attention to the careers of cults themselves.

Chapter 5

THE STAGES OF CULTS

It is clear that people go through changes as they enter cults, adapt to their doctrines, and perhaps take their leave of such religious groups. Cults themselves have careers like the people who belong to them. As people have reasons for joining and leaving, cults have reasons why they become successful as a species of religion and why they may fail. To understand the concept of cults this supra-individual level must also be examined, although as yet no one academic treatment has adequately covered this topic. This perspective also suggests that the impact of cults on modern America and, for that matter, the world of history, is even broader than suspected. This is because we should add the existence of the many failed cults to what we know of those which have been more successful!

How can we gain an insight into this cult perspective? One key study by an anthropologist, Anthony F. C. Wallace, is helpful in this respect. This author has compared a great number of cults to see if defined stages occur which are all shared in common. And, indeed, he has determined five basic cult stages for those cults which do achieve success; stages broadly applicable to the career of any cult. These stages also fit nicely into what has been previously discussed relative to cult behaviors on the individual level. He begins with a stage he calls the "steady state." This represents a baseline for the development of cults. In it, the vast majority of people in a society or subgroup are relatively content. This is to say that "culturally recognized techniques" exist for need satisfaction. These may be represented by orthodox faiths or other alternatives. Stress occurs of course but remains, in light of the above, within tolerable limits. Perhaps nobody can be pleased with life all of the time.

The next stage is represented by "increased individual stress" in the population isolate under scrutiny. This is due says Wallace to less efficient ways of dealing with stress which is caused in turn by changes in that group. These changes might then be broadly those of the relative

47

deprivation nature discussed previously precipitated among tribal peoples (a focus for Wallace's study or by military defeat and related disorders introduced by the spread of Western civilization). Such changes could be internal within our own society as well. At any rate, the consequence is a rise in stress levels among many people in the population. If such events continue, conditions reach the stage of "cultural distortion." The elements that make up the culture of the group in question, especially its stress-relieving mechanisms, become inadequate for a majority of people; the previous harmony of life is shattered. Life has become inconsistent in its satisfactions. Stress continues to rise although it is responded to differently. Some individuals try to tolerate higher stress levels, some search about and try limited changes in their lives, still others regress, becoming apathetic or worse. Disillusionment occurs in all cases. Are Slater's comments on American society relevant here?

As cultural distortion rises, the society is ripe for what Wallace calls the stage of "revitalization" (he calls cults "revitalization movements"). A prophet arises, Moon, Meher Baba, or a tribal leader as discussed in later chapters. The prophet is a person who has restructured the way of looking at the problems of life. Whether by insight or revelation this prophet combines various elements in a new way to provide stress-reduction possibilities. He or she then communicates this non-orthodox message by identifying with this new view of life and be under supernatural protection. Benefits to society in general may also occur. Remember the Moonie doctrine and that of the Hare Krsna in this respect! The prophet gains first converts who become "disciples" and help spread the message. Organization also develops at this stage. As more converts are made, the cult begins to assume the leader—inner circle—follower form so common to many such religions. Think of the ashrams, orgs, and other groups previously discussed.

As the organization grows larger, the key to revitalization and cult success intrudes into the picture; the cult must adapt to the surrounding society as it exists at that time. For tribal peoples this may mean overcoming or getting along with the powerful, dominant Western presense that originally increased the stress levels to cultural distortion levels and triggered the rise of the cult. For us it would be the overcoming of family, church, and political responses. Adaption may involve such things as deception, force, modification of doctrine or whatever. Failure in adaptation means that the career of the cult could be reversed or severely inhibited relative to further growth and influence. Recall the case of the Divine Light Mission! Other examples of failure in adaptation are given in this and subsequent chapters. If adaptation is successful—and no two cults may face the same adaptive problems or work on them in exactly the same fashion—then further revitalization can occur resulting in cultural transformation. As numbers of people come to accept the cult, the culture becomes less distorted and members experience reduced stress. The cult has an effect: for tribal peoples perhaps reuniting the whole group; for moderns a more limited effect on the population isolate involved—the closed cult society itself. Group action is organized, hopeful, and, at least for members, productive.

If all these phases occur—rise of prophet, communication, organization, adaptation, and cultural transformation—then revitalization on some level has been achieved and stress has been reduced. If this state of affairs continues to exist over a lengthy period of time, the group and its formulations become a part of the status quo, part of the normal "cultural scenery." The group has made a place for itself in the world. Since cults wish to maintain that place, there now occurs what Wallace calls reunitization. The organization has the preservation of doctrine and stability of ritual as its main goal. The cult wishes to keep what it has laboriously achieved and becomes church-like in many respects. If this is all successfully done, then the last main cult stage develops: the "new steady state." Society or its involved part is back to "business as usual"; conditions approximate those prior to the stage of increased individual stress. Some scholars have suggested that the Hare Krsnas may be approaching this point at present.

Wallace's study suggests how cults may develop and the circumstances that evoke such developments. Other studies have taken more specific approaches to the growth of these new religions or to the success factors involved. In the present brief chapter we can look at two of these studies. The first is by Rodney Stark and William Sims Bainbridge as part of their general book on the nature of the cult phenomena. In it they suggest some ten factors that can promote or limit growth and success after the origin of a cult. We can look at several very crucial factors these authors cite. They remind us that growth rates themselves are crucial as a cult develops. Specifically, a cult must grow at a very rapid rate each year if it is to "catch on" and become significant within a few generations. As an example, if a cult begins with twenty members and has an annual growth rate of 10 percent—which sounds successful—in ten years the cult numbers only fifty-two people and after fourty years only slightly more than nine hundred! In a large society such as the United States this may in fact mean that they have no significance at all. The Moonies, who are generally judged as one of the more successful cults, did begin with about twenty members back in 1962 but expanded to over 6,000 by 1980: a 40 percent growth rate. That spells success and they certainly did receive attention from the wider society!

A second of the many factors suggested by these authors is closely related to the above. This is the relationship between growth and hope. It is possible that when growth is slow in a cult, for whatever reason, the existing members may lose heart, having worked hard and having achieved little or nothing in terms of social impact. The leader has aged as have the early converts. They will not live to see success even if it does eventually arrive, so they must experience a sense of failure. And, like the Bo and Peep cult, they may be stimulated as a result to change the message and/or turn inward. Stark and Bainbridge do suggest that this is why many cults do shift to the form of an "elect remnant of believers" who may isolate themselves from the very mass of potential converts necessary to make their new faith a success. The result becomes a kind of self-fulfilling prophesy for failure.

Still speaking of the "people" factor, these authors also remind us that some very elementary aspects relative to the growth of cults have to do with the nature of their target populations. Clearly, not all members of a general population can be recruited into a cult to make it grow and become significant. Those who are fairly strongly committed to an orthodox faith (over half the United States population) and those who do not accept the notion of the supernatural as viable in problem-solving ways are already off limits as potential members; so also are those who are too deeply committed to the values of the secular society. Since cults generally tend to reject society, those who are too deeply committed to its values would have much to lose by joining such a religious group. Remembering our statistics on who joins cults, we should also rule out most of those who are fairly old or who are preteens! If you wish your cult to grow and be successful, you will certainly encounter difficulties in the all-important recruitment numbers game! Add to this the fact that your cult has to compete with other cults who also need members and, as previously discussed, the fact that not everyone stays in a cult anyway. Perhaps fewer than 10 percent of Moonie recruits actually go the distance to full cult involvement. So, the potential for unproductivity is great in this key area of cult growth and development.

A last factor we can highlight from the list of these authors is the role of charisma—a favorite sociological topic in the general study of religion. For a cult to get started requires a leader or prophet as Wallace has suggested. To be a prophet whose message is taken up by disciples and others requires a person with great ability to attract others; to make the message plausible however "far out" that message may be. He or she must convince followers of a special truth and apart from the attractiveness of the words his own character must attract people through personal magnetism. This is called charisma and one suspects that its lack in a potential founder has doomed many potential religious groups to oblivion despite other potential prospects for success. Nor is this the only problem related to the prophet. He or she may be very successful in recruiting members, but as the new religion grows the many organizational needs and "inside responsibilities" may take this unusually gifted person from the streets and the cutting edge of recruitment. Busy with management the prophet cannot be as involved in other cult matters, and in the absence of equally charismatic followers the growth of the cult may decline after a promising beginning. This may especially be so inasmuch as many recruits have personal problems which may occupy much of their time. Meeting their own needs rather than recruiting others or having inadequate skills to apply to that task may undercut the viability of the cult in terms of the factor of recruitment and ultimately work against overall success. As Stark and Bainbridge conclude, "prophets do not entirely control their own destinies" in these respects and they compete for a small pool of people; requiring in Wallace's terms certain cultural distortions to perhaps even attract these. It seems somewhat incredible that as many cults develop and survive as they do!

Luther Gerlach and Virginia Hine have also suggested factors that contribute to the success of cults. They are primarily interested in how a religious group becomes a true movement of transformation that implements personal and social change. This makes their perspective congruent with aspects of Wallace's revitalization. These authors focus primarily on Pentecostals and the Black Power movement, but their insights apply nicely to the types of religious groups discussed in this book. As they see it, there are five key factors which make such groups successful. These are organization, recruitment, personal commitment, ideology, and opposition. We have already discussed some of these from the point of view of individual conversion. Now we wish to examine them from the vantage point of the cult. Some overlap occurs with what has already been said in the present chapter, but these authors do point out some new and important ideas.

Organization, of course, was a phase suggested by Wallace. Gerlach and Hine suggest a model for success in these respects. Among other things, a cult that will grow and have longevity should have a degree of decentralization with many local groups—ashrams, orgs, or whatever they may be called. While all such units are held together by ideology and common behaviors, they are spaced out geographically and real membership and ties are on this local level. This also suggests that while there may be an overall leader or figurehead, a Moon, Maharaj Ji, or Meher Baba, these local leaders are the day-to-day influences on the lives of the followers of the cult. They may even innovate with respect to recruitment and other matters on local levels. The local groups are also held together by leaders across unit lines. Sannyasis among the Hare Krsna, regional directors, and the like keep local groups from deviating too much.

These authors suggest that while such an organization may be seen to lack form and overall organizational unit, it nevertheless is very adaptive in at least four ways. First, in dealing with the wider society (Wallace's adaptation), maintenance of security is important. With many local groups the "establishment" would find it more difficult to counteract the cult or suppress it, as "they are everywhere." Likewise, if new leaders are required, there is a constant supply of experienced personnel from the various local groups. This may not be ideal for replacing higher-level leaders, but it makes it difficult to harm a cult by "cutting off its head." When Moon was in prison, the Moonies did not wither away and die without his direct control! Having many groups make up a cult is also ideal for spreading the cult across many geographic areas. Perhaps part of the failure of Bo and Peep was to keep their members essentially altogether. Both in accommodation to the wider society and in terms of drawing in new members the more local groups and innovations possible, the more a variety of ways exist to pursue the goals of the cult, the more likely it will be a success. One group doing its thing in one way cannot be as flexible as a number of groups each adopting perhaps a little different strategy to fit local circumstances. Finally, here, failure is minimized. The loss of one group for whatever reason does not end the movement; the other "cells" continue. The infamous People's Temple Movement of Jim Jones concentrated most of their members and leaders in Jonestown, Guyana. When the group committed mass suicide in anticipation of government intervention, the movement died out for all intents and purposes.

A second factor in cult success is recruitment. We have discussed this at length previously. It will suffice here to mention that from the cult-success perspective, the key to recruiting is face-to-face contact between highly committed members and potential members, and it is suggested by these authors that the contact be made on the basis of pre-existing ties between these individuals: trying to recruit someone into the movement with whom you have a social tie. This notion is somewhat in contradiction to the idea that people suffering relative deprivation will naturally join cults, but many specific studies have suggested that pre-existing ties are most important. Perhaps these maximize such needs. We need more research along these lines!

The third factor is personal commitment. Here, along lines previously suggested from the individual convert perspective, cults need to generate some act or experience that separates the new convert from the outside world and changes his or her behavior along lines valued by the cult. This would be the bridge-burning experience that makes it difficult to return to the outside world and gives the converts the single-minded assurance that the cult will provide everything in their lives. Remember Kanter's discussion of these points! If a cult fails to provide a clear alternative to the established order, if it fails to gain the complete allegiance of its followers, it is less likely to grow and be successful.

The fourth factor is ideology. This of course provides the conceptual framework for the other factors. It defines the outside world and that of the cult, it defines the special "truth" of the cult and provides the focus for commitment. How is a cult more successful than others in these respects? While cult beliefs are different, Gerlach and Hine suggest that the effectiveness of ideology derives less from its meanings or even appeal than from the certitude it manages to convey to its believers. It is less what is believed than that something is believed; that it is firmly transplanted into the heads of cult followers! The followers must become so sure of the answers provided by the cult that complete dogmatism and the patterned response of the "party line" become automatic. One should wind up fanatics who will accept no other view and will allow nothing to deter them from their goal; people for whom even failure is seen as a test or even as a kind of success! So it's less a question of the message that leads to cult success in terms of this factor. It would be interesting to see if some types of ideology might be easier to transmit in this fashion.

Finally, there is the factor of opposition. Gerlach and Hine suggest that a cult will be more successful than others if it can build up a "psychology of persecution" in its members. Whether actual or invented and from society in general or from local officials and others, members need to feel that the "world is against them." Among other things, this motivates their efforts, gives them a sense of wellness, and creates the dividing line between themselves and the world so necessary for cult success. Of course, if that opposition is real and very strong this will work against the cult as has been the case in many tribal religious movements discussed later on. A little but not too much seems to be the watchword here! Having very briefly and incompletely examined these factors, along with earlier concepts, we can now examine a specific case of failure.

Stark and Bainbridge give an excellent case of at least the partial failure of a recent cult in the United States. A discussion of this can illustrate some of the above points and conclude this brief chapter. The failure of some other cults will be discussed in later chapters. The cult in question, paraphrased from the study of the above authors, is Transcendental Meditation; TM for short. The name of this cult will be familiar to most readers. It began much like Scientology as an effort designed to upgrade the effectiveness of the lives of those who embraced its teachings and techniques. It was begun in the United States by Maharishi Mehesh Yogi and claimed a following at one time of more than half a million.

The early success of this cult stemmed from its claim to be able to increase a person's energy levels and mental clarity. This not only enticed persons with real needs along the lines we have previously discussed but drew the attention of businessmen, students, and others looking for an edge in their activities. Famous people such at the Beatles became attached to its techniques, with subsequent publicity for the cult, and articles in even scientific journals were at first lauditory of its accomplishments. Maharishi spoke at universities, and even earlier in time UCLA college students had formed an organization to spread the gospel. Clearly, a movement was well underway with a prophet, followers, and an effective organization—one non-threating in its organization. These were all ingredients for cult growth and success!

A person "joined" this cult and received its benefits by attending a couple of free lectures by adepts to learn about its concepts and values. Ultimately, the movement wished to transform society, to make an "ideal society and an age of enlightenment." Then a person enrolled for instruction in meditation techniques. This required payment of a variable fee. This was all pretty straightforward, although the adept would perform a minor rite of thanks to the Hindu tradition from whence the basic meditation aspects were drawn. A personal mantra was also given to the student as an aid in focusing the meditation. This was supposedly secret and tuned to the student, although it turns out these were drawn from a rather limited list. After these techniques were mastered, the initiate attended a number of meetings to share experiences with others and so get reinforcement. Remember "I see Baba in you." They could also receive extra help at this time. While one could always go to a local TM center, it seems most people simply went on their way aided by this newfound edge in life.

In the event one wished to become more of an adept and to gain even more knowledge, weekend retreats were held with discussions and yoga exercises which were said to "intensify clarity and energy," to work better than the usual twenty-minute meditation session. Religious elements drawn from devotional Hinduism were also added at this point and applied to everyday life. In addition to a rapid proliferation of TM centers by 1972, the Maharishi International University had been founded. This not only was the center for TM doctrine and technique but offered new versions of traditional academic subjects based on the ideology of this movement! It sent catalogs, received students, and granted degrees. By 1975 the cult had reached a high point in terms of members, although only a relatively few, perhaps 6,000, had become full-time devoted members and teacher adepts. Revitalization seemingly had occurred for followers and the future success of the cult seemed assured.

In the next two years, however, a precipitous drop in new converts occurred together with diminished interest among many previous initiates. It is hard to determine quite what went wrong at this point. Many new cults offered different opportunities for growth to the seeker/searcher types who formed much of the TM clientele. The results of life improvement so enthusiastically predicted often failed to materialize. Scientific journals also became less than positive at this point. Fees were raised and this in a small way may have been an inhibiting factor for some prospective members. Certainly a lack of full-time control over the lives of most members made defection easy and knowledge of competing cults more obtainable. At this point an interesting parallel to the career of Scientology developed. The cult introduced a more mystical element: the concept of the Siddhis. Siddhis were persons who could develop supernormal levels of consciousness; becoming invisible, flying through the sky, and knowing the future. These and other claims were coupled with the announcement that those who entered the university could qualify for these courses. Clearly, this was a device to lure back the early levels of converts or keep the faithful, but this new element certainly made the claims of the cults more difficult to verify and easier to discredit. It also brought negative public response to what had earlier seemed to be an innocuous meditation technique; it was now recognized as a religion and one of the far-out cult variety! The result was to further reduce membership and attractiveness. In light of the earlier discussion of this chapter the certitude of the message and the adaptiveness of the cult were no longer present. And, losing much of its vitality, the movement remains restricted at the present time; much reduced in membership and influence. We can now examine the types of cults and attempt to get a sense of what overall differences in structure, belief, and emphasis that may occur between them.

Chapter 6

THE TYPES OF CULTS

We have examined only a few of the hundreds of cults that exist in the United States today. Still other cults exist elsewhere in space and time—geographically and historically. Despite some communalities as discussed in Chapter 1, they present a bewildering variety of types. This is true not only with respect to beliefs and practices but with respect to all aspects of them: size, recruitment methods, hold over individual members, and the like. Is it possible to make some order out of such disorder, to neatly divide cults up into a number of highly similar types? Can we arrange them into a useful taxonomy? The answer is probably not! Certainly no consensus has emerged and no one scheme has emerged that appears satisfactory to a majority of scholars. Nonetheless, if we understand that the purpose of any scheme of classification is to help us to order our data and to suggest research possibilities, and if we also remember that such schemes are a working model for reality and not that reality, then it is worthwhile examining a few such schemes for the potential insights that they can offer. We will also discuss such schemes as applied to tribal peoples since we are about to turn to such examples in later chapters of this book.

Willa Appel has at least a hint of a classification in her book. It is very limited but does suggest a dimension of cult differences on which a classification might be constructed. In her view cults can be compared in terms of how much control they are able to bring to bear over their members. She makes a dual distinction as a kind of polar opposite scale along these lines. *Totalistic* cults are those that do attempt to control all aspects of the lives of their followers. They are in sociological terms totalistic institutions in ordering the beliefs and lives of members. In her words they exert great pressure for conformity and force members to sever ties with their past and with the outside world which is viewed as evil or satanic. Such cults also force members to give up independent ways of thinking and activities; all of life is directed along the lines of the cult. Such total immersion in this type of cult is usually, she suggests, accompanied by mind-altering activities such as chanting and meditation. Generally, such totalistic groups involve withdrawal from the world, or at least live-in arrangements along the lines of the ashrams previously discussed. Jonestown, the Hare Krsna, and the Bo and Peep cult would likely be examples of this form.

At the opposite end of the scale would be *non-totalistic* cults. This type would exert much less influence over its followers. Most such persons would still live and work in the world or secular society and retain at least compartment of mind and behavior outside the cult framework. The advantages of the cult would meet the needs of members without absorbing their full time and energy. Transcendental Meditation and some levels of Scientology would probably fall here. Many cults would be placed somewhere on the scale between these two extremes. Appel also suggests that cults can be classified in terms of their ideological content: their belief systems. Perhaps wisely, given the great diversity here, she does not really attempt to provide us with a scheme along these lines. Her distinction between totalitarian and non-totalitarian cults is however valuable in a limited way. Control over the individual member as a potential facet of every cult and the degree of and presence of virtual absence of this is easily recognizable and attributable. Yet, we should ask if a classification based on only one character is useful beyond a level of merely examining if other characters also pattern along these extremes as well.

An example of another rather limited scheme is that of Geoffrey K. Nelson. His criteria of choice for classification revolves around how a cult comes into existence and develops. This is an approach quite different from that of Appel. Nelson really has two classifications. First, one can classify cults in terms of the dynamics of their origins. In this case two types emerge: *charismatic* cults and *spontaneous* cults. In the former case, cults form around the figure of a leader, some person with a dominant and charismatic personality. It is the individual magnetism of this leader who attracts disciples and eventually lay members regardless of what the advantage of the cult is to the followers. We are talking here about Bo and Peep, Meher Baba, and Maharaj Ji, among others. Spontaneous cults, on the other hand, develop, in Nelson's words, from an informal gathering together of people having similar experiences, ideas, and interests. Seeing that they share a great deal in common in at least a vague supernatural sense they form a group or groups to pursue a life-style, or whatever, along these lines. A good example here is the so-called Church Of All Worlds.

This cult developed in the late 1950s and 1960s among a small group of friends who became infatuated with the ideas of the philosopher and novelist Ayn Rand. To her works they added the influence of the psychologist Abraham Maslow relative to his ideas of self-actualization. This notion coincided somewhat with the hero conception of Rand. Later, after reading the science fiction novel *Stranger In A Strange Land* (Robert Heinlein), whose extraterrestrial being had super attributes, these friends resolved to develop for themselves and others a life-style and system which would create human beings with god-like potentialities. By 1967, the Church Of All Worlds was founded and began the creation of local groups—nests—to accommodate converts among whom the phrase "thou art god" reflected the supernaturalistic dimension and higher consciousness of members. While the figurehead of this cult was Tim Zell, no one person or point of view ever dominated it and the cult is basically extinct at the present time. It is (was) however an excellent example of the spontaneous variety of cult.

Nelson's second classification relates to cults on the basis of their careers. If they have just begun, they can be called a *local* cult. If they have managed to reach Wallace's phase of organization, then they are called a *permanent local* cult. Certainly, by this time they will be larger and be better equipped to promote their message and to face societal responses. They have now achieved a kind of publicity level. Finally, if they go beyond this point and develop much wider appeal, if they develop local branches, ashrams, orgs, study groups, or whatever, they become what may be called *centralized* cults. This last type will vary depending upon whether or not its origins are charismatic or spontaneous! This classification in terms of development is probably more useful to a student of cult careers than to people interested in cults in general. The first pair of distinctions is quite useful, and one gets the intuition that charismatic types will probably also be fairly totalitarian in Appel's sense and spontaneous cults much less so!

Another example that is rather equivalent in scope to the first two is that provided by Stark and Bainbridge in their excellent general book on cults. As they see it, there are three degrees of cult organization. These degrees are suggestive of degrees of control but not in terms identical to authority. First, there are *audience* cults. In this type of cult organization the "members" gather to hear lectures and perhaps discuss related matters, but there are few if any aspects of true group organization. As these authors neatly put it, the cult behaviors fall more along the lines of a consumer activity. Books and magazines are read, conventions held, and benefits derived but mostly on a part-time and somewhat vicarious basis. Cult behaviors are largely passive!

An interesting case of this type of cult is the Amalgamated Flying Saucer Clubs of America. This was one of many groups arising in the 1950s and 1960s during the presumed flying saucer sighting years. This organization was founded by Gabriel Green who had been contacted by an extraterrestrial from the planet Clarion (often by phone) with messages for humanity. Some of these messages he related were also revealed to other contactees. As in other such groups, the messages basically were aimed at saving us from ourselves: requiring economic and other reforms and often suggested that UFOs would intervene directly in human affairs. Various periodicals which also detailed life on other worlds were sent to members, many of whom also attended conventions of like-minded people. Except for the occasional get-together, most members of the cult went their own way with only literary contact with the leader. This and other UFO cults, it may be added, have declined severely, as have the sightings of such non-earthly vehicles.

The second type of cult in Stark and Bainbridge's classification is the *client* cult. In this type of group the leaders and disciples are highly organized, but the members (clients) are less so. The members still remain in the secular world and maintain previously existing ties and commitments. They do, however, more actively derive benefit from the cult's advantages. As in Scientology, members get cleared, or they become more functional as in TM, or they come to realize the aid of Meher Baba in their life successes. The most active level and intense organization, however, is that of the *cult movement.* Here, members meet regularly with the cult leadership and do sever their ties to all other institutions. Their goals are also beyond immediate and personal benefit. They want to bring others to "the knowledge" and effect social changes. The Moonies and Hare Krsnas are examples of this type of cult organization. Again, one assumes the totalitarianism criteria rises as one approaches this last cult type.

One of the most interesting attempts in recent years at the classification of cults is that of Bryan R. Wilson. His approach is to create a typology for new religions that covers both cults and sects. He examines them from the perspective, not of organization or career, but in terms of their main social orientation towards the world. He asks how people in these groups feel they can relate to the world in terms of gaining salvation. It is, of course, taken as a given that the responses engendered by these groups are of supernaturalistic forms.

As Wilson sees it, there are eight such responses, the first of which is a baseline (like Wallace's steady state) for considering the other seven. This baseline is called the *orthodox* response. This is the most dominant salvation technique in society and accepts the world as it is. It sees no real evil in the world and the values and goals of the culture are accepted as mostly legitimate and the religious system backs them up. This position represents that of the mainline churches previously discussed. All the other responses can also be ranked in terms of how much they withdraw from and/or reject the world and its values as well as the vehicle they employ for salvation. For a ranking in these terms the reader may wish to consult an article by Michael Welch cited in the Bibliographic Essays at the end of the book. My presentation will focus on how salvation works and gives the seven alternative approaches in a slightly different way from that of Wilson.

All seven alternative approaches see at least some degree of evil in the world and suggest a means for overcoming it. The first of these is the *conversionist* response. Religious groups of this type, sects or cults, consider that evil does exist in the world, but it exists there because evil is in us, in people. The outside world is corrupt or whatever because people are that way. The key therefore is to change people! If we can do this, get ourselves transformed, then the world will change as well. What it takes says Wilson is a change of heart. Salvation is by a supernaturally aided transformation of the self, an emotional transformation. One wants to say, "I lived in sin, but now I am pure." This whole process takes a new orientation in the subjective sense. God can change us even if it takes some work by ourselves. The proof of being changed and of having left evil behind is seen in the conversion experience itself: by being "born again." Clearly, members of such groups will display little interest in political and other solutions to social problems, since it is, after all, a question of change of heart. The reader will recognize this to be the stance taken by some Christian evangelical groups: the born-again Christians.

The second response taken is the *manipulationist* approach. These groups see evil as fundamentally in the world itself rather than in humans. Evil is external to themselves, although they can certainly be affected by it. Thus, they seek a new, non-orthodox way of dealing with that evil. Evil can be dealt with and salvation assured if humans can learn improved techniques (manipulations) for dealing with it. Since there is more evil than can be dealt with in a regular fashion, new religious perception is required. God calls upon us, says Wilson, to change our way of looking at the world and our means of dealing with it. We can avoid illness, poverty, and other deprivations through the new perspectives provided by these groups. It should be added that these groups may be fairly accepting of the world as it is although less so than in the orthodox response. They nominally accept the world and secular goals. They merely change the supernatural means of achieving them! Christian Science is usually cited as an example of a religion of this nature.

The third variety is that of *thaumaturgical* sects and cults. This and the next variety assume a very active supernatural and perhaps, correspondingly, more powerlessness against evil in the world on the part of humans. Salvation here is largely wrought by God through specific miracles rather than by new principles or manipulations to follow per se. It is magical in operation and holds out the possibilities of experiencing some kind of contact with the supernatural. This may be for healing, a better job, knowledge of the future, or other God-aided relief of deprivations. Perhaps in the long run thaumaturgists merely believe they have obtained guarantees of life after death through their membership in such groups. Excellent examples of this type include many of the Caribbean cults of Afro-American ancestory dealt with in the next chapter. Such may be the cults of the truly oppressed! The fourth type as indicated above is very close to this one. It is the revolutionist response. Here, the sought-after miracle from God is a big one! God will overturn the world and the evil that is in it. Only the destruction of the existing world and social order can save us. And this destruction, despite some human input can ultimately only be wrought by God through supernatural means. Cataclysm and catastrophe followed by restoration of a perfect world lacking evil is the ultimate goal. Many tribal cults fall into this category, for example, the Ghost Dance and some Cargo cults. The Christadelphians are generally cited as modern example.

Wilson labels the fifth type of religious response as *reformist*. This and the next type involve much greater activity and impact by humans. The Gods may help us here and give some direction, but miracles and supernatural transformations are generally not part of the picture. In a reformist group the notion is that God has called upon humans to alter part of their world; to reform or amend the world as revealed in some manner. Evil is in the world as in other cases, but it is not so pervasive or intractable that humans with supernatural revelation cannot deal with it. This is, as Wilson points out, close to secular humanist positions which reminds us that non-supernatural kinds of techniques for dealing with evil may overlap significantly in belief, technique, and orientation to religious movements. Unitarians are often cited as an example of this response.

The sixth type goes the extra mile with respect to reform and stands in contrast to it much as revolutionist does to thaumaturgical. It is the *utopian* response. Here again, by revelation God calls upon us to reconstruct the world. A little reform is not proof against the evil of the world; only a new social order and organization will be sufficient to eliminate it. Obviously, this type of group response is very close to the exact opposite of the orthodox acceptance of the world. Here in rejecting it as "too evil to deal with in pieces," it, like the revolutionist approach, seeks a major overturning of things as they are. In the utopian case, however, humans have to actively restructure the world. Generally, this occurs by setting up a utopian type of community apart from the world which is seen as a device or model on which the world can be eventually remade. The Oneida community of central New York State in the 1800s was a fascinating example of this type of response.

The last type of response rejects the world and its evil to perhaps the highest degree. It is the *introversionalist* response. Here again there is too much evil in the world to deal with in ordinary terms, but rather than God or humans changing the world the technique for salvation here is in withdrawing from the world in the fullest possible sense. Salvation comes from renouncing the world and maintaining social isolation in a separate community as have the Old Order Amish and other groups. Here the withdrawal is not done to form a model for changing the world in the future but to achieve purity and freedom from evil and so achieve salvation in the present. Withdrawal becomes a defensive reaction! God calls upon us here to abandon the world.

The approach to new religion classification by Wilson in terms of orientation to the world and type of salvation is potentially very useful. As has been pointed out, there is an overlap between his types that makes clear placement of any specific group a matter more of degree than kind. All cults have a degree of utopian community. But if we see it as a matter of main emphasis, this classification does represent a very useful device.

It is also one he applied to tribal religious movements. If all religion involves transformation and salvation, perhaps the best way to examine cults is along these very lines. We can then see if some types, say revolutionist, are more likely to be cult movements or audience types, more or less charismatic, or whatever! It is also necessary, however, to introduce more anthropological classifications at this point; typologies devised to deal more specifically with cases of tribal cults. We can now turn to this perspective.

Anthropologists who study tribal societies have discovered many cult movements in the general sense that Stark and Bainbridge use this particular term. The majority of such movements have arisen in response to pressures from contact with more powerful societies, chiefly those of the Western world. In contrast to what we have termed the relative deprivations that motivate cult membership in this society, the above impact is generally one of more total deprivation for tribal peoples. In response to cultural distortion in Wallace's sense, the resulting deprivations are certainly real and involve a greater proportion of the society in question. Such have been called the religions of the oppressed. How much tribal and modern cults really have in common is a matter that has not yet really been explored. Clearly, however, they share much in their genesis, history, in departure from orthodoxy, and even in specific behaviors. It is therefore relevant to include such data in this book. We can examine several anthropologically inspired classificatory schemes in this present chapter and then examine specific cases in the next two chapters, even extending our examples to include some from non-tribal societies.

One of the oldest attempts to categorize tribal cults was by Ralph Linton back in 1943. In his view such religions only developed in response to outside pressures and were responses to those pressures. As predominantly Western, stronger societies impacted on a tribal society, the latter began to lose its cultural identity and experience cultural distortion. A cult would then arise which Linton called a "nativistic movement." This attempted to revive that culture or at the very least perpetuate aspects of the culture. This would represent an organized effort in Wallace's sense, and the aspects selected to revive or perpetuate would be those of a symbolic nature and/or those that were distinctive with respect to the more dominant outside culture. In short, the group involved is aware of an outside culture and feels its own existence is threatened and attempts to rectify this situation.

Linton believed, based on the above considerations, that there were two main lines along which such nativistic attempts might develop. In the first of these he distinguished between *magical* nativism and *rational* nativism. In magical nativism the people involved rely heavily on supernatural mechanisms which involve miraculous and unusual events that will occur for the participants. This might involve resurrection of the dead ancestors of members or the sudden disappearance of the outside people causing the problems the members have encountered. As such, magical forms of nativism present strong correspondences to Wilson's thaumaturgical and revolutionist responses! Rational nativism still involves supernatural mechanisms, but these are chosen more "realistically." The beliefs are less far out and unverifiable and make fewer assumptions which can be negated by the actual state of affairs. Again, in Wilson's terms, these movements fall more along reformist and perhaps manipulative or conversionalist lines. They may even be content with the development of some rite that provides solidarity and a sense of accomplishment for the threatened group.

The second line of development for Linton involves whether the movement is attempting to actually revive certain aspects of the culture or is interested in (or only capable of) perpetuating those aspects. In the first case the emphasis is retrospective. Its focal point is on the past in wishing to bring back at least some of the "good old days." In the second case, perpetuative nativism, those involved attempt to preserve aspects still retained in the culture before these too disappear, especially things that set off their culture from others. If we take both lines of possibility into account, we can derive four basic sorts of movements: magical revivalistic, magic perpetuative, rational revivalistic and rational perpetuative. On inspection of the data from tribal peoples it turns out that nativism falls rather definitely along the poles magical revivalistic and rational perpetuative, which does, I suppose, have a certain logic. In fact, there are few, if any, clear examples of magic perpetuative cults. At any rate, this is a classic scheme for sorting tribal movements even though it did not, unfortunately, leave open the possibility that the deprivations or whatever that cause them might be of an internal rather than of an external nature.

A more comprehensive anthropological classification is represented by an attempt by Marion W. Smith who called such religions cult movements rather than nativistic movements to expose a wider focus. Such cult movements are felt to be organized and deliberate as in the case of

Linton's scheme and to originate as responses to social and economic dissatisfactions. This clearly allies them to the types we have previously examined. This author also assumes that stresses are involved and changes, not necessarily limited to the sphere of religion, will be part of the outcome of such movements. Since change is involved in some manner; Smith proposes that these new religions can be divided up in terms of this basic aspect. *Nativism* seeks to revive or perpetuate aspects of a particular cultural system. It draws on internal resources so to speak. Might this be a sect-like cult? Vitalism places more stress on external sources and utilizes newly perceived aspects of culture brought in from the outside. Such seems fairly congruent with Eastern cults in the United States. Smith sees (and remember we are talking about tribal groups here) vitalistic movements as more progressive and those of a nativistic nature as more regressive, especially in terms of growth and other potentials. A last form that cult movements may take is *syntheticism* which stresses a combination of "ingredients" taken from both external and internal sources.

In the Smith scheme, then, the scope for such movements is wider than that of Linton in terms of the genesis change being within, without, or both. Comparable to Linton's mechanisms or lines of possibility, this author also points out that any type of movement will have certain contextual features or possibilities. A movement may, for example, stress the coming of a messiah or savior and it may stress the arrival of a cataclysm or a new-age type of event. A movement may involve militancy on the part of members who seek change through the vehicle of force (and the destruction of old or new behaviors) or it may have reformative aspects of more limited motives. Finally, such activities may display revivalism, "excessive exhibitions of personal behavior," such as wild dances or trance. It would be interesting to see if such elements fall along the lines of magical or rationalistic; if they correlate more to revivalisms or perpetuations in Linton's sense.

Many writers have pointed out that cult movements by tribal peoples in the sense that they are tied to change, the improvement of conditions, and related matters are really a special form of social movement. While the means they employ are supernatural, they share many features with movements of political, economic, and other basis. This is a more specific observation related to the oft-cited notion that religion in general shares much with other realms of behavior. It is also clear from the cult movements we have examined in the United States that such observations are not limited to those of a tribal nature even though the most noticeable and overt expressions may be found there. Ideally, then, a scheme for classifying religious movements ought to merge with those of more secular natures.

David F. Aberle, an anthropologist, has offered a limited approach in this direction. His overall category of data is called social movements and he sees these as organized efforts made by a group of people to bring about change in the face of resistance by other people. Somewhat like Linton, he organizes his divisions along two lines of cleavage: the location of the changes sought and the amount of change desired. In the first case, the location or focus of the desired changes may be on an individual level or may be on the level of society; effecting change in some major institution or all of them; "clear" the whole world or bring it together under the banner of the Unification Church. In the second case the amount of change desired may be partial or total. Does the movement desire to change just a little or rework things more completely? This is like Wilson's reformative versus utopian categories! These two lines of division then intersect to give us four categories into which social movements may be classified.

The first category, total change on a societal level, Aberle calls a *transformative* movement. Like the utopian, revolutionary and magical revivalism types previously discussed, its attempt is to change everything on a social system or societal level. Such types often involve heavy doses of supernatural activity as we will see in the next two chapters. Secular revolutionary movements would also fit into this category even though they may lack all reference to religion or downplay it. Aberle's second type is called a *reformative* movement. This approach aims at only a partial change in society and so these are much more limited in scope. These often appear to have less supernatural aspects even if the movement itself is religious, and these often take purely secular forms; for example, the woman's rights movement today. The third type, movements that aim for total change in individuals, are called *redemptive* movements. The attempt here is made to effect behavioral changes more by the creation of a new inner state by psychological and other means. Conversationalist and manipulationist responses of Wilson's typology probably fit here. Again, this variety of social movement can be largely devoid of supernatural content; witness psychoanalysis which is surely a search for a new inner state and redemption. The final variety in this scheme is the *alternative* movement. This aims at only partial change on the level of the individual, and a secular equivalent might be the birth control movement. It is Aberle's feeling, one very supportable, that many of the tribal movements studied by anthropologists fit into the transformative and redemptive categories. We could say the same thing for our own society, although some new religions fit all of these categories in all of the schemes we have presented here.

The reader is probably very confused at this point since we have examined several ways of classifying cults, none of which are quite equivalent. Each, however, highlights some useful distinction we can draw if we wish to contrast cults to see if other correlations follow. And there is noticeable overlap between some of these categories. Remember, too, that such categories and schemes are to help order data and provide stimulus for research. It should also be understood that such schemes are ideal classifications; no cult may fit perfectly in them! Likewise, we should keep in mind the notion that cults may change their character over time. They can go from a client type into a full-blown cult movement (in Stark and Bainbridge's terms) and perhaps change from redemptive to transformative in nature as they do so. These categories do have usefulness despite the various classification approaches that exist. We can now turn our attention once again to descriptive materials by examining cults, predominantly tribal, elsewhere than in the United States, in space and time. These materials will enable us to see how anthropological or other categories apply and give us a sense as to whether modern and tribal cults really represent comparable phenomena. We return to theoretical issues in the last chapter.

Chapter 7

THE AMERICAS

We can begin our consideration of cults elsewhere in space and time with a review of a few such movements among various North American Indian groups. It should be mentioned that this chapter and the next chapter are more descriptive in nature and are intended to provide a comparative perspective. Native Americans are a classic case of the assertion that tribal cults develop in response to outside pressures that cause social and economic difficulties. American Indian cults also display the revive-or-perpetuate aspects suggested by Ralph Linton, since tribe after tribe was disrupted, dislocated, or destroyed. When Europeans arrived on these shores they were characterized by three motives, all of which worked against the interests of the native populations they encountered. A lust for wealth led to the plunder of many groups or their enslavement as workers. Wars between European powers were also carried to the New World where various Indian groups were recruited as allies or were caught in the middle. And, finally, religious zeal in converting the "savage" took away major props to cultural integrity, this at a time when many Indians were in disarray. To these motives can be added greed for the land itself which led to the greatest problems of all. Settlers poured onto Indian lands displacing former inhabitants by any means possible. All of this was compounded by the impact of European diseases which decimated many groups having no natural immunity to them.

Throughout the course of such activities, some of which continue up to the present time, many attempts were made by populations of Native Americans to reject or accommodate to the encroaching Europeans. When military efforts failed these attempts took the form of religious movements, the forms of which fit nicely into the various cult schemes discussed in the previous chapter. And, in general, such cult movements have fallen along the lines suggested by Linton for tribal cults. The first phases of Indian-White relations in North America were rather revivalistic.

Movements reflected a desire to recover Indian culture which was rapidly being lost. Here the past offers the salvation of native culture, in that it could be salvaged by religious means. Much magical behavior was involved here. The more recent contact phases spawned movements calling for adaptation to non-Indian ways, since indigenous patterns clearly could not be resurrected. Such movements stressed religious independence but borrowed many outside elements and were essentially rationalistic in character. Change and progress were more important than a longing for the past. We can briefly survey a few of both forms of movements.

One of the most dramatic examples of the first type of movement that appeared in North America was the Ghost Dance. Many Western peoples were involved in this cult which first appeared among the Paviotsos of Nevada in 1870. Among these people it was begun as the prophet Wodziwob. He had received a vision in which he saw a railroad train carrying Indian ancestors who were returning to life and who would announce their arrival with a great explosion. In this vision it was also suggested that the world would witness a great cataclysm and then it would open up to engulf the Whites who would then disappear. Their material wealth, however, would somehow remain for the Indians. Even the Indians would die in this upheaval, but those who followed the new religion would be reborn shortly afterward and live in the company of the Great Spirit in an eternal existence. The basic ritual consisted of men and women dancing around a pole. The dances performed were mostly traditional types, but the songs dancers performed to accompany them were new, having been taught to the participants by the prophet Wodziwob who had apparently learned them during his vision experiences. We see a strong magical component here and the type of cult that Wilson labeled revolutionist.

This early phase of the Ghost Dance had, for the most part, only a local significance, although it did spread to a few other societies. Perhaps its major impact was to stimulate a number of other such movements, most of which also predicted destruction, resurrection, and the removal of Whites, and had somewhat new ritual activities designed to hasten the appearance of such events. Around 1890 a new and more potent phase of the Ghost Dance arose under a new prophet, Wovoka (John Wilson). This caused a very widespread expansion of this cult. Wovoka was a Paiute and he had been some sort of supernatural leader among these people. His own vision was gained during a period of sickness, which is common among such prophets everywhere. His phase of the cult was originally a little less hostile to Whites, although their ultimate removal was greatly desired. James Mooney gives us the best account of this movement and characterized its doctrines as follows. At some time in the near future all the various Indian peoples, both living and dead, would be reunited upon a regenerated earth. There they would live a life of happiness as in the old days and be free from death and disease. The whites would be left behind and not be a part of this future, as they were not a part of the past. Such a desired state of affairs was to be brought about by an overruling spiritual power—one that required no help from humans to accomplish these things. However, all believers were admonished to make themselves worthy of this future by embracing good moral behaviors and to live at peace with the whites. As before, the suggestion was that the dead were shortly to return and that this would be announced by cataclysms. Immortality would be the reward of the faithful.

As suggested above, part of Wovoka's doctrine consisted of a code of ethics. Injunctions were placed upon harming others and on lying and stealing. Followers of the cult were told to love one another, to work hard, and to give up some of the more destructive ritual aspects of their old religion; for example, destroying property as a sign of mourning in death rites. This emphasis did go against the military focus of some groups, and in fact some groups who became followers added the notion that the special shirt worn in the cult, the Ghost Shirt, had supernatural properties that could protect the wearer against the weapons of white soldiers. Some active resistance followed as a result!

As in the earlier phase, the major ritual endeavor in 1890 was a special dance which occurred over a four- or five-day period. Men and women danced in concentric circles. Leaders invoked the ancestors in an opening song and were then joined by other participants who often numbered in the hundreds. Other songs were sung as the dancers circled around the pole. During rest periods between song and dance performances leaders would relate their own vision experiences and engage in sermonizing activity relative to the ethical aspects of the cult. As the dancers continued their movements the level of excitement slowly built up until some participants were swept away by the emotional aspects of the endeavor, much like Hare Krsnas. Such excitement was enhanced by the leaders who attempted to stimulate and "psyche up" such people even further. Eventually, such persons would break out of the circle and stagger into the ring and pass into a trance-like state. In it, they like the leaders might have a visionary experience and communicate with the supernatural world. While some temporary positive effects were gained from such dances, feelings of hope and solidarity, ultimately such magical supernatural efforts were doomed to failure. The dead did not return as promised; whites did not disappear.

Another example of a cult along the lines of the Ghost Dance was that called the Cult of Dreamers. This was founded by the prophet Smohalla, meaning "preacher." This movement came into existence among groups living along the Columbia River in Washington and Oregon around 1860. Groups in this region were refusing to move onto reservations provided for them since they feared that to do so would confine them for further assimilation into white society. At this time many cults of a local nature were developing, and these along with that of Smohalla were attempts to provide hope in the face of increasing white pressures. As in the case of Wovoka, this prophet also claimed to have had special visions. He had been a shaman among his people, the Wanapum, and in such a capacity he had engaged in a fight with a rival who had defeated him and left him for dead on a stream bank. Rising waters carried him downstream where he was rescued by a white farmer. After a lengthy period he recovered and then traveled widely throughout California and the Southwest before returning home. When he did arrive there he proclaimed to everyone that he had died and that he had met the Great Spirit, or supreme being. This God was unhappy that Indians had taken over white culture and had allowed their own traditions to lapse. If people would return to some of the old ways, then God would remove whites, return the lost lands of the Indian, and resurrect the dead.

Smohalla's faith was called Washani ("worship") but became referred to as the Dream Cult after his own designation as the Dreamer. This was due to his frequent trances in which God revealed certain knowledge to him. This information was then passed on to his followers. His theology included the notion that the creator had made the Indian first, after which came other peoples—French, priests, English, and so on; all in turn from each other. As Indians were first in creation, the only God-created beings, therefore the earth belonged to them! Furthermore, the earth itself was a goddess who should not have her breast plowed; farming as well as other white customs becoming a sacrilege. Farming was also a wrong behavior, since it was from the soil that the dead would rise again once they were reanimated by their souls at the time of a cataclysm.

In this cult, wisdom clearly came in visionary dreams, but there were also regular ritual activities. These began with a procession of the faithful from a cult house with the leaders carrying a banner with symbolic decorations. Smohalla also wore a special shirt. After the procession, the worshippers returned to their cult house, went inside, and arranged themselves along the walls with the prophet in the corner. There was a verbal recitation of dogma and singing and dancing accompanied by drum music. These latter activities as in the Ghost Dance eventually led to trance behavior in many participants, culminating in dreams which could then be told to fellow worshippers. Special rites might also occur, the most common being a Salmon Dance and a Berry Dance held as in the past to mark the start of these wild resource seasons.

The message of Smohalla gained a number of converts for this cult for a while. In 1877, the Nez Perce Tribe was even stimulated into military activity against whites. Eventually, however, this cult wained, its message did not come true and followers lost interest. Smohalla died in 1895 and was succeeded by his son, Yoyoumi, and then by a nephew, Puck Hyat Toot, whose death led to the final end of a severely declined faith. We can now examine a pair of Native American cults of a more rationalistic bent which still survive at the present time.

A religious movement still found among modern Iroquois is the Handsome Lake religion. Named after its Seneca prophet, it is also referred to as the New Religion and as the Gai-wiio, or "Good Message." This movement began among one band of Indians along the Allegheny River in western New York State in 1799. These people, along with other Iroquois, had been severely impaired by effects of contact with whites. Prior to the end of the French and Indian War (1763), they had maintained their power, lands, and much of their self-esteem. With the British victory in that conflict they could no longer play off the two sides against each other. Later on in the Revolutionary War most Iroquois backed the British and as a result their heartland was devastated by the triumphant colonies and their population was greatly reduced in numbers. The ultimate result led to confinement to reservations with a number of grim consequences.

For the Seneca, specifically, most of their land had been alienated by 1797 and they were greatly impoverished. In June of 1799, Handsome Lake, the brother of a local leader, received a vision. Like other prophets who found cults, he was sick and near death at the time. Recovering, he reported that he had been visited by three angels who told him they had been sent by the Creator to show him how to get well and to tell his people about a message. He was to report that the Creator was angry about evil practices that were going on. These included the use of alcohol, witchcraft, and love magic and related practices. People who were guilty of doing things said the prophet must admit their wrongdoing and repent. Confessions of such sins could be made to Handsome Lake or, if truly bad, to the Creator.

The prophet reported this message during a ritual that was being held and added that rituals of a traditional nature were also supposed to be continued as in the past. Several weeks later a fourth angel appeared to Handsome Lake and he thus had a second vision. In it, the prophet was taken on a spiritual journey through heaven and hell and he was given a moral code at this time. This was accomplished through a number of scenes in which he saw various types of evil persons and the punishments they had received. Clearly, witchcraft, promiscuity, wife beating, gambling and the like were behaviors that were causing trouble for the Indians and the angel told Handsome Lake that they had to cease. The Seneca prophet again recounted his vision. In the following year yet a third vision occurred. The three original angels appeared and urged him to carry on in his role as one who should spread the good message. His health continued to improve and he did found this new religion and gained many adherents. He had further revelations and died in 1815.

A close student of this cult, Anthony Wallace, sees two major strands or "gospels" involved in it. The first of these was complete at the end of the third vision. This gospel was apocalyptic and continued three themes: the world would soon come to an end, sin had very specific dimensions, and there were steps that could be taken for salvation. If the Indians did not cease their bad practices and return to traditional religion, the prophet himself would die and then the earth would be destroyed. The specific sins had been cataloged in the visions and to these were added the failure to believe in the Gai-wiio! Release from sin and gaining salvation was accomplished by following the path laid down by Handsome Lake. Confessions of sin as previously mentioned was the crucial element here.

The second gospel, a social gospel, followed these teachings. Along with an emphasis upon moral conduct, these teachings suggested (quite rationally) economic and technological efforts such as learning how to farm in a White manner and no further alienation of land. Ultimately, this gospel had more to do with revitalizing the Seneca and providing them with social stability. After his death he was succeeded by his nephew and then other leaders. His message is preached and recited at the mid-winter festival on various Iroquois reservations in New York and Canada at the present time. A written code was determined and composed early in the present century.

We can examine a final case of a North American Indian movement, one that again continues to the present time. It is also the most widespread of such nativistic endeavors. This is the Peyote cult or Native American Church. This movement basically seeks adjustment to Whites rather than struggle against them and a return to the past. In this sense it is a more rational supernatural effort. Its focal point is the use of peyote in a ritual context. Peyote is a small carrot-shaped cactus which contains narcotic alkaloids. In early times the Aztec and other peoples ingested the plant ceremonially, either in the dried or green state. The use of the plant produces "visionary" experiences which give the plant its obvious religious values. Its early use was as a therapeutic and hallucinatory device: for curing the sick and offering protection as well as alleviating fatigue and as a bridge for contacting the supernatural world. As its use spread into North America, it was incorporated as part of a religious movement in response to White domination and became popular about the time that the influence of the Ghost Dance was waining. In fact, its first prophet, John Wilson (not the man previously mentioned), was introduced to peyote at a Ghost Dance and had a vision. In it, he went to heaven and met various supernaturals. He ultimately was informed that God had put part of the Holy Spirit into peyote for use by Indians. He was also taught songs and other ritual aspects. Wilson then started the cult and adopted a strict ethical code to go along with it. As the cult spread, many offshoots and other prophets developed; many with a heavy Christian theme, some more aboriginal in nature. Eventually, many were loosely merged together (1918) as the Native American Church. Since cult practices do differ somewhat from one group to another, we can focus on one example, the Taos Pueblo Indians of New Mexico.

At Taos Pueblo, unless sickness or some emergency is the cause, the rite is performed on a Saturday night. It is held in response to the vow of an individual and such declarations are made for three main reasons: to gain a supernatural solution to some problem, to show appreciation after its solution, or to gain general blessing and good luck. The person making the vow becomes the sponsor of the rite and must provide food, invite participants and select a leader. A tipi as a ritual structure must also be erected and other material paraphernalia obtained and readied. Other leaders must also be selected: a fireman who tends a ritual fire, a man who places cedar incense upon it, a special drummer, and a woman who is in charge of water and who brings in a ritual breakfast at the appropriate time. She is often the wife of the sponsor. Preparation by other participants who are all male and who number perhaps fifteen individuals at any rite is variable, but there is a general feeling that behavior should be circumspect on the day of the ritual. Certainly alcohol must not be used.

Ritual procedures run as follows. The participants gather in the early evening and the fireman goes into the tipi and lights the fire which is a part of an altar complex. Others line up in a special order, with the male leaders first. A prayer is offered by the main leader and they all enter the structure. The cedarman places incense in the fire for purification and the peyote is warmed by it. Tobacco is passed which is made into cigarettes whose smoke can be "prayed through." At this time a formal prayer is offered in which the purpose of the rite is stated. Portions of peyote are then distributed to all the participants and ingested by them, ultimately to produce visions.

The leader sings a special "starting song" accompanied by the drummer. Singing and drumming are then also done by the other leaders and by those participants who wish to do likewise. Prayers are also said privately during these activities. At midnight the leader again sings a special song and water is brought in and passed around. The leader goes outside and prays and upon his return the singing, drumming, and individual praying continue until dawn. Most visions seem to occur at this time, visions interpreted by participants as contact with and reflecting special protection from the supernatural world of God. When it is almost sunrise the leader again sings a special song and calls for water. The water woman enters with the water and after some ritual activity she prays—also relative to the specific purpose of the rite. The leader offers another formal prayer at this point and the female leader leaves and returns with a special "breakfast," which, like the water, is symbolic of the necessities of life. Food and water are passed out to participants and after consumption the leader sings a special "quitting song" and participants file out of the tipi. Most remain in the area until noon when a special meal is served to finally terminate the ritual activities.

As one can guess from this very brief description, the Peyote cult rite is an extremely personal kind of experience. One derives from it pretty much what one wishes. As many members have stated, it is a kind of road that one can follow. The experiences provide direction, help in times of trouble, and a sense of exclusiveness; only members (Indians) qualify for such benefits. This latter notion is certainly typical of the cult experience everywhere! At Taos Pueblo the cult goes beyond these variable functions. It is in this village a kind of middle ground for religious experience between the older faith now rapidly declining and Christianity which some pueblo members do not respond to as positively as others. Older people long for the Indian past; younger persons wish to be brought up to date. Peyotism is demonstrably Indian, but it is new rather than aboriginal in nature, so in it the old and new are integrated together. The cult reinforces their collective sense of social and cultural identity and helps to preserve their morale. It has helped, in other words, to solve at least some of their social dissatisfaction problems. And like all of the cults mentioned so far in this chapter, whether magical or rational in Linton's terms, it does offer hope to the oppressed, to those who feel deprivations.

What about such cults elsewhere in the Americas? In Central and South America and especially in the Carribean there are a great number of cults which fall into one or another category as discussed in the previous chapter. Some are ongoing movements, others of these religions seem to be dying out or are extinct at the present time. Some are similar to North American manifestations; many are unique as a class to these religions. Here, not only were the Indian populations oppressed, but groups of African descent, originally imported as slaves, also suffered greatly. In these cases many people experienced deprivations of various types. At the peak of the slave trade to the New World (1700–1810) over nine million human beings were imported here, most outside of North America. Since these lived under harsh conditions it does not surprise us that great potential existed for the development of religious cults; for the religions of the oppressed which promise aid for their followers. Such is still the case today for blacks, Indians, and other minorities.

The classification of the resulting cults is uneven in the literature that relates to them, and the interested reader will want to consult Bastide and Simpson in the Bibliographic Essays at the end of this book. Here we can merely point out typical elements which many such cults exhibit. First, many of them provide members with visions or direct contact with the cult deities as a way to gain aid and overcome problems. Trance states of leaders are particularly notable. Second, many are derived in some way from traditional African religions which may also blend in Christian elements; the kind of blending of elements so typical of cults in general according to some writers. Such syncretistic cults are perhaps the best known. Finally, many emphasize anti-white feelings and express strong political yearnings which may relegate religious elements to a more secondary position. We can briefly examine three specific examples for comparative purposes. These are the Convince cult which has been fading since 1950, Santeria which after many years is still spreading, and the Ras Tafari which is also experiencing growth.

The Convince cult is in Jamaica and is also called the Bongo cult as a term of derision relative to its African origins. It originated among slaves who had escaped from their owners during the sixteenth and seventeenth centuries (Maroons) and who eventually won their freedom. They continued to live in isolated areas and developed a reputation for spiritual powers. Such powers are believed to come principally from contact with ancestral spirits of former members of the cult. Some spirits are very strong, having come from Africa as slaves (where it is believed the cult originated), others are the spirits of born slaves, still others derive from the ghosts of recently deceased members. One can secure aid from all of these various types of Bongo spirits, although the power involved ("Obeah") can be good or evil.

The Bongo spirits decide who will become a member of the cult through visions or actual possession of such a prospect. It helps if one is already a lay member or sympathizer. A spirit may have many devotees and a person may have more than one spirit. The relation is initiated because the spirit wishes a body so it can sing, dance, smoke, drink, or whatever, offering those it possesses protection, good fortune, and aid in working Obeah in turn. This last can result in income that can help economic deprivations. The help such leaders or Bongo Men can give to others, cure illness, insure success in various endeavors, has an obvious appeal for many who are not selected by the spirits directly.

This cult is very informal in organization, with single leaders living scattered about the countryside and leading their own rites for their own groups of followers. This is clearly a client-cult type as discussed previously. Individual leaders often attend each other's rites, but some competition also exists since each wishes to gain the reputation for contact with the strongest spirits. Each leader has assistants called *grooms* who are leaders in training and a variously sized group of followers called well-wishers who also assist and are given "discounts" when they need Obeah worked for their benefit. Many are devout Christians but see the Convince cult as a different arena for spirituality; one that has magical properties. Rituals occur in non-calendar fashion. Most commonly, two or three Bongo Men put on a public, nightlong dance and associated activities for various reasons, often only to give new ghosts an opportunity to possess new devotees. Annual sacrificial rites are also held, lasting several nights, to keep the spirit contact secure and to give feast for supporters. Special rites by single leaders for the working of Obeah also occur followed by public rites which include offerings to the spirits involved.

Ritual activities typically run about as follows. Invitations are sent to other Bongo Men and lay persons who might wish to attend. On a Saturday a pavilion-type of structure is set up in the yard of the leader's house and a consecrated spot to which the spirits will come first is designated. This is symbolized by a pole, flowers, table, candles and related paraphernalia. Visiting Bongo Men and their clients arrive and add their candles and other objects and are served rum and marijuana. A kind of Christian prayer meeting starts off the evening activities as a way to let other spectators know that the rite is about to begin, and about nine o'clock the leaders come out from the house and begin to dance individually to a series of songs sung by well-wishers which are intended to call the spirits.

The spirits now come one at a time and "mount and ride their human horses," the Bongo Men. At first, such persons thrash about and try to deny their possession, and the groom assistants have to assist their leaders as those persons propel themselves around the yard on the ground, like a real groom hanging on to a real horse! A groom eventually pulls his leader to his feet, making sure that the possessed Bongo Man does not run away, as this would lead to permanent possession. After a while the possessed leader quiets down and assumes a contracted position with hunched shoulders and bent knees and is dressed with a special shirt and headdress representative of the spirit involved in the possession. The spirit now speaks words of greeting through the mouth of the leader and begins to sing and dance. Between dances the spirit (leader) walks about the yard and converses with well-wishers in a strange dialect. He drinks rum and smokes, as this is the joy spirits take in inhabiting their human alters. They may also engage in other, often comical, activities. After a time the spirit leaves. The Bongo Man shakes or starts, acts confused, and then becomes himself again with no apparent memory of what transpired while he was possessed. Bongo Men follow each other in being possessed and the series may last long into the night. If sacrifice is involved, a goat will be beheaded and butchered as an offering and feasting will occur.

This whole ritual activity is entertaining for onlookers, many of whom are first drawn to the cult in this context. Beyond this the acts reinforce the potential powers of the leaders of the cult and the spirits in the minds of members; powers that may accrue to their clients. Obviously, humans and at least these spirits can interact on the same plane of reality, with material benefits filtered through the human end of such relationships. The working of Obeah through such persons can cure the sick, insure successes in love, harm enemies, help one secure a job; in short, work any manner of miracle a deprived person may desire. In addition, the fellowship of belonging to the clientele group of the Bongo Man and the wider association when many people gather for the rites, meets needs for belonging and dependence; that desire for community commented upon previously. Convince is clearly a cult in the functional terms of Scientology, Meher Baba, and others with which we are already more familiar.

A movement which operates very much like the Convince cult is Santeria. This terms comes from the Spanish word for saint, and in this cult statues of saints up to five feet high are believed to really be West African (Yoruba) divinities. Possession of adepts by these deities parallels the ancestor possession of the Bongo Men previously described. This being the case, in presenting this cult I will emphasize the process of becoming a member rather than ritual activities. Santeria developed in Cuba and Puerto Rico and has spread to Florida and New York City. We thus observe here a cult which is still actively providing assistance for its members. It began as a cult like others as a response to colonial oppression.

Santeria members believe that a person is assigned a protective African spirit called an Orisha at birth, and if one can discover the identity of such a being and become initiated into a relationship with it, then a great success in life will follow. Santeria leaders called Babalawo can bring this relationship to fruition. In addition to contact with one or more such deities, the initiate will learn proper manufacture of various magical objects, potions, and spells which can also aid in pursuing various desirable goals; these include harming one's enemies, getting a job, and other endeavors similar to those mentioned for Convince members. But the gods are the most important and potent aspect of this cult.

Many deities exist and each has a favorable sacrificial animal, herbs to give refreshment, stones on which blood is spilled as another form of sacrifice, and related connections such as color associations. Of the many such separate spirit entities that exist, seven are grouped as the "seven African powers" and are considered most important. These are as follows. Obatala represents the heavens and is a god of purity, excellent for removing evil influences. Eleggua, more of a trickster type, opens roads and doors and so is always invoked before other deities for whom, so to speak, he opens the door. Chango (Shango) is a god of fire and thunder and is a verile deity for passion and also for dealing with enemies. Oggun, a god of metals and war, is excellent for employment and gaining wealth as well as for fighting illness. Yemaya, a sea goddess, is considered the mother of many Orishas and thus is invoked for human fertility and woman's problems in general. Orunla is the great god of divination and his adepts can predict the future and discover hidden knowledge. Persons with him as a patron receive a full set (18) of divining stones instead of just a few as in the case of relations to the other deities. Such people can do only partial divination. Finally, there is Oshun, the goddess of love and marriage. Her gifts are obvious. Hundreds of other deities also exist.

A number of steps are necessary if a person decides that he or she wishes the aid and protection that such spirits have to offer. Initiation is a long and costly process, much like that of a well-wisher becoming a groom and eventually a Bongo Man in the Convince cult. The first step is to find a sponsor, generally a Babalawo, who can determine by divination the identity of one's own Orisha. The novice then receives one or more protective bead necklaces of different colors representing the deity or deities in question. Five to seven necklaces are usually worn, since protection comes even from spirits with whom one has not predetermined connection. Collectively, the necklaces stand against all kinds of evil that might befall a person. As such, they are almost never removed. Surely, if a person has deprivations of almost any kind the notion that protection is available in such tangible form can help provide a new outlook on life. Though on a lower level this is doubtless like the reassurance of knowledge sessions in the Divine Light Mission. The necklaces are presented to the novice in a special ritual and must be purchased, at no small cost to the generally impoverished would-be member.

The next step in becoming a member, which requires further mone-
tary investment, is called the "Making of Eleggua." Since this deity
opens the way to others, his aid is necessary for deeper levels of supernatural contact. Therefore, the leader prepares a one-foot sculptured
head of this god out of cement and other materials. This sculpture is
vague in appearance but nevertheless represents the god and is kept by
the now further initiated member near the front door as protection
against any enemies and to serve as a link to other Orishas.

The major ritual of initiation is called Asiente—"making the saint."
This is in keeping with the god-saint overlap of this and related cults.
This brings the novice into direct contact with his Orisha and as a
possessed person gives the capability to work with other such beings as
well. The cost is enormous to the initiate: about four thousand dollars!
The rite occurs in some special location sacred to Santeria and involves
the novice, sponsor, members, and the main leader of the local area.
Many ritual maneuvers occur and no two rites are exactly the same,
although they are generally comparable. The following events may be
taken as fairly typical. There is a cleansing of the head of the novice
since this is a prime "contact" area. Magic paste is used and is left on over
night. The head is shaved and color circles are drawn on it which
represent the associated spirits. Colored robes complete this symbolism
and are worn by the novice. Sacred drums are beaten to invoke the
concerned spirits to arrive and to possess the novice, and after a time that
person goes into a trance state and eventually collapses to the floor.
During the unconscious interval that follows it is believed that the power
to be a conduit for spirit power develops; the initiate is transformed to a
more than human level.

Several other rites now follow. A cross is made with a razor blade on
the tongue of the still only semi-conscious initiate and an herb mixture is
put in his mouth to secure blessings from the Orishas. The sponsor kills
a chicken and offers the initiate some of its blood to drink. The initiate,
now fully conscious, is seated in a special chair and observes a number of
animals sacrificed and partakes of the blood of each. He then remains in
the sacred place for several days eating special foods and being washed
with special magical potions for purification. Two more purification
rites occur, three and then six months later, and the initiate has become a
full-fledged member of this cult. He can now participate in all rites, have
spirit contact, do some divination, and perform other essentially magical
deeds for himself and others.

The new status of cult members helps social deprivation, and the new skills have economic as well as self-esteem value. In other words, Slater's desire for community and engagement motives are clearly met as are many of the more specific relative deprivations of other authors. Certainly, the Santeria, as in the Convince case, provides that personal encounter with the supernatural that Cox feels is lacking in traditional faiths. We can hardly conceive of an encounter stronger than possession! So the motives that attract young Americans to the Krsnas or the Divine Light Mission seem much the same as those that promote membership in Santeria. We can now examine one final example of a cult from this geographical region; one orchestrated in a somewhat different direction.

The Ras Tafari is an avowedly political cult which originated in Jamaica in the early part of this century. It is unique to that island, although it has spread to parts of the United States. Members of this cult who are mostly lower-class blacks believe that a black messiah appeared to redeem them from the many oppressions they have suffered at the hands of white people. This black messiah represented Africa as the promised land of redemption; Jamaica, meanwhile, was the biblical Babylon of captivity soon to pass away.

The main impetus for this cult was Marcus Garvey, who founded the Universal Negro Improvement Association in 1914. This group offered hope for the improvement of blacks. His intentions were to develop mechanisms to educate blacks in their cultural heritage as an aid in improving their self-image and status. He also planned for a world brotherhood of black peoples and the development of Africa into a modern "nation." This would galvanize oppressed black peoples along the above lines. Unfortunately, Garvey was basically unsuccessful in this in Jamaica due to White and upper-class black opposition and so he left for the United States in 1916. When he left, he admonished his followers to expect the crowning of a black leader in Africa. This man would be the expected redeemer.

In 1930 such a person, Ras Tafari, was crowned king of Ethiopia. He took among his other titles the name Haile Selassie (might of the Trinity). This galvanized new leaders to attract followers in the slums of Kingston and a vital religious movement was soon underway. It was a movement that involved much militancy against the establishment, and at times members had to flee to communes in the mountains to perpetuate the cult. In 1960 a government study of the cult led to an understanding of the more practical improvement aims of these groups and somewhat more tolerance. This corresponds to Wallace's phase of adaptation. However, actual conditions are not much better today.

What are the main beliefs of this cult? Rastafarians believe that Haile Selassie, who died and assumed a spiritual body in 1975, is the living god of the black race. He was really Jesus, the biblical messiah, but white peoples have hidden this knowledge from blacks so they could keep them in subjugation! The God of white people is the Devil; thus the problems in the world today. Blacks are a holy people since they are a kind of reincarnation of ancient Israel. So they had to live in "Babylon" for their sins. These sins have long been expiated, but white oppression has delayed their return to the promised land. Jamaica as Babylon and hell will be replaced by Ethiopia as heaven and blacks will be repatriated to that location and will eventually rule the world as a superior race of people. Prior to this desired event a member becomes a son of God and gains eternal life. Here, we are clearly dealing with a messianic type of cult; in Wilson's terms, one of a revolutionist nature.

This cult is motivated along political lines and does have a ten-point moral code designed to strengthen the intellectual and behavioral resolve of members. Its provisions promote brotherhood, racial consciousness; in short, many of the notions originally suggested by Garvey. It also objects to the use of sharp objects on the body as in shaving and haircuts which has led to dreadlocks—wild hairdos symbolic of Ethiopian warriors as a virtual badge of membership. Members also use a potent form of marijuana (ganga) as a mark of belonging and as a protest of the status quo. It is also used as a kind of sacred element. Rastafari is weak, however, along the ritual lines so typical of such religious movements. It has been pointed out that members rely more upon faith than works!

There are weekly or monthly meetings by members to discuss current problems and future promises. These begin in the evenings and may last into the night. A special prayer by a leader opens each such meeting and basically recapitulates the hoped-for miracles. Drumming and dancing occur after this, often interspersed with much smoking of ganga which is thought to aid in meditation and "visions." The prayer is recited again at the conclusion of the meeting. Scholars suggest this cult is presently reaching a kind of routinization stage, "as much organization as prophetic message." Certainly many members are working hard to appear respectable. This suggests that some revitalization, some need satisfaction has taken place. We can return now to other world areas and cults that have appeared there.

Chapter 8

THE PACIFIC, ASIA, AND AFRICA

A veritable host of cults exists from areas of the world outside the Americas. Some occur or occurred in traditional tribal societies; others developed among more complex groups of people or are currently functioning in modern nation states. All of these cults fall into the classification previously discussed and came into existence for the reasons we have already cited. The present chapter merely highlights a few of the more representative of these movements. A complete and chronological exposition would require an entire volume. The Bibliographic Essays at the back of this book suggest a few more comprehensive materials relating to them. We can begin our presentation with examples drawn from the area of the Pacific Ocean.

Tribal people of the Pacific have always fascinated anthropologists with their cultural variety. Such cultures have also been, in Wallace's sense of distortion, impacted by a number of influences from the outside. From the 1500s through the 1700s, explorers poked among these islands, although their disruptive influences were generally minimal. In the next half century or so, traders, whalers, and missionaries had much greater impact with new goods and ideas, especially in the latter case. Planters and slavers (blackbirders) partly dominated the next time period (1850 to 1914), often severely harming local societies and causing heavy deprivations. Nation states vied for spheres of influence and colonies in the early 1900s, and World War Two in its Pacific manifestations added to such difficulties. In Linton's terms the original inhabitants were surely peoples ripe for nativistic and other cult movement expressions, and even today these continue to be developed since many groups have not achieved real independence.

Some of the best known of these religious expressions come from the island of New Guinea in the part of the Pacific known as Melanesia. Here, as elsewhere, many cults originally began due to the stimulus of missionary activity and teachings. One of the earliest here, in 1893, was the Milne Bay Prophet Movement. This cult was founded by a young man by the name of Tokeriu, who apparently was possessed by a tree spirit in more or less traditional fashion. He had some sort of visionary experience like North American prophets and claimed to have visited the "other world" and prophesized that in a very short period of time a great storm would come bringing a huge wave which would cover the entire coastline. All would be destroyed, but Tokeriu's fellow villagers could be saved if certain things were done. Most practically, the village should be moved inland and rebuilt in new style with houses in long rows and a house for the prophet built separately. In revivalistic terms, European goods were to be repudiated and followers of these teachings should wear special decorations as a sign of such rejection and the anti-European attitude which accompanied this cult.

Tokeriu further claimed that after the new village weathered the storm, crops would multiply in the gardens and a ship would appear manned by the spirits of the dead who would disembark and be reunited with their living relatives. The ship would remain under the control of the prophet. Such magical elements were very attractive to followers; all the more so since Tokeriu was to form a government independent of Europeans and with the ease of gardening little work would have to be done. In fact, the village was built and existing food stocks consumed. Adherents did begin to wait for the expected cataclysm. Unfortunately, as in cases of extreme magical nativism, disillusion soon set in accompanied by pressures from missionaries and other Europeans. The message of the prophet was seen to be false and he himself was jailed, as much to save him from his angry followers as anything else. This cult did not reach a stage of revitalization, but such movements did occur elsewhere in Melanesia, perhaps influenced by the Milne Bay activities.

Such a later and also unsuccessful movement first occurred in 1919 in New Guinea and was referred to by missionaries as the Vailala Madness. This cult was begun by an older man, Evara, in the village of Vailala apparently after hearing a missionary sermon on resurrection. Sometime later, and perhaps with such a notion in mind, he had a trance experience after the death of several of his close relatives. This experience resulted in prophetic revelations of the same sort as those of Tokeriu. The basic message presaged the arrival of a boat which would bring back dead ancestors. It was believed that these revived individuals would also bring back with them the "cargo": crates of European goods intended for the followers of the prophet. Somehow, Europeans would leave and in fact an early notion later toned down was that part of the cargo would be rifles to hasten this process. It should be mentioned that ships bearing goods and sometimes ancestors were widespread in this Pacific area and are collectively referred to as Cargo cults in the anthropological literature.

In this cult, the ancestors sent messages and perhaps power to leaders. In some villages this was accomplished in the following manner. A flagpole would be set up and leaders would stand at its foot receiving messages and inspiration from the dead as if from a European radio set antennae. Other leaders received their information by staying for a time in the cult dwelling called a "hot house." In all cases, messages came down, went into the stomach of the leader and then out through his mouth in the form of essentially meaningless singing. This verbal element was accompanied by a swaying of the body and rolling of the eyes. These emotive behaviors would then be taken up by followers through emotional contagion (or by pretense) until whole villages were dashing wildly about. Hence the name Vailala Madness. The native people apparently called the movement "head-he-go-round belly-don't-know" and the leaders became known as "Head-he-go-rounds." At any rate, the knowledge or power was placed in the leader's stomachs by the soon-to-return ancestors.

There were other aspects to this cult in addition to the more flamboyant emotionalism. Mortuary feasts were very important. These were performed by cult members to honor the dead and took new forms; older rites of this sort were banned. Tables were set up in European fashion with flower decorations, and followers would sit at or near these for long periods of time while abandoning work in the gardens. A formal ethics was also generated reminiscent of that of some American Indian movements. Rules here included prohibitions on adultery and stealing, the giving up of some older ritual customs, no personal adornment, and keeping the village clean. Rules also encouraged the taking up of a number of European customs even though followers sought no accommodation to these powerful outsiders.

This cult, despite its magical overtones (their ship never came), did survive longer than the Milne Bay expression. By 1923, however, its more emotive phase had passed. The leaders did retain control over villages, but real credibility was maintained with only a dwindling number of real followers. Revitalization did not occur. To maintain themselves the "Head-he-go-rounds" carried long poles and went throughout villages "carried by the divinatory power" of these poles and knocked down huts of verbal unbelievers. Thus, they used fear to perpetuate their status. As they became older the cult simply faded away, dying out in the next decade.

Another cult reported on from the area of Melanesia is called Marching Rule. This is the anglicized rendition of Maasina Rule which means the rule of brotherhood. This movement occurred among the Kwaio and other people on the island of Malaita in the Solomon Island chain in the late 1930s. It was a cult with some definite cargo implications, but, like the Ras Tafari example discussed in the last chapter, it had heavy political implications.

For many years after contact, slaving had depopulated much of this island, and even after the establishment of a British administration, the native people were indentured workers on plantations engaged in copra production. While these people were influenced by European culture, using tobacco, working with steel tools and the like, they did not regard Europeans with awe as better people and they did not give up all of their traditional culture. The Kwaio also regarded other islanders with whom they came into contact as representing a common heritage. In the 1920s heavy missionizing had succeeded in making some converts and causing bitterness among traditionalists. Even earlier, bad feelings had developed over British interference in blood feud settlements and other native politics. Resentment among the Kwaio led to attacks on ships and the massacre of a district officer and party of tax collectors. This in turn led to strong countermeasures: the killing and arresting of natives and destruction of gardens and villages. By the mid-thirties, resentment and deprivations were rampant.

Earlier non-military alternatives had occurred on the island. For example, in 1921 a Cargo cult was manifested, but its failed prophesy had only led to mockery and conversions to Christianity. In 1937, however, among the Kwaio, an ancestral spirit possessed a man called Noto'i and spoke through him to the effect that American troops and ships would arrive and displace the hated British. Houses should be built for the soldiers and the goods that they would be bringing with them. People who wished to benefit from these events should also live within a special area and give offerings to the spirit revealing this information. It is possible that this message was partially inspired by the earlier presence of two American naturalists who had spent a month in the interior of Malaita and by stories about an American plantation manager in the southeast Solomons (called Diki Merika) who had created an almost mystical image about himself. At any rate, many people did destroy their houses and rebuild them in the sacred designated area. However, the prophet was arrested and the predicted invasion did not occur.

In a sense, reinforcement of the prophesy did occur during World War Two with the invasion of Guadalcanal and other activity in the Solomon Islands. At this time, Malatians not only served as labor gangs for the invading Americans but encountered the huge amounts of goods that they brought with them. Some of this "cargo" was shared with native peoples who were also treated very well. Likewise, the Americans were triumphing over the Japanese, whereas the British had been driven away. Such notions crystallized in the cult called Marching Rule in 1944. It developed in several areas and on Malaita with leaders such as Nori and Timothy George.

What was the message of this cult? Its most overt aspects were political. Leaders wished to organize the island under native political control from regional chiefs down to local leaders in a fashion parallel to the colonial-imposed system. This would include such leaders having armed body-guards and other assistants to regulate garden work. This was seen as a way to unite kinship groups, pagans, and Christians alike under a common rule of brotherhood to achieve collective goals. To facilitate such union, local groups were to be brought together in larger villages along the coastline. This would also enhance farming projects and communication possibilities. All customs were to be "codified" and only criminal offenses would be subject to European disposition. Leaders sought better working conditions on the plantations and equality of treatment, including better medical and educational services.

The British at first accepted much of this as reasonable. But in a few years more militant leaders, who had hoped the Americans would throw the British out, had begun to threaten British life and property. They had also by this time attracted almost all of the native population to the cause of the movement and large meetings accompanied by mass hysteria were occurring. Along with all of this were religious aspects of a cargo nature.

Part of the religious message of the cult at least hinted that the Americans (who had left) would return again with their ships and that these vessels would be filled with goods for followers of the cult. Goods included items like those in earlier trade stores and post exchanges during the war years. Such goods would be stored in huts and given free as gifts to cult adherents. Those persons who were not members were to be driven back into the jungle. Storehouses facing the water were built to receive the goods in some areas. Not only did such events fail to come to fruition, but, because of the fear engendered by the political aims, the British eventually felt the need to vigorously respond with a program of repression. They arrested the leaders. By 1950 the unity of this cult had been broken and those who clung to its notions had been splintered into more local movements.

The political content of the Marching Rule cult in the Solomon Islands in Melanesia has often been found in native cults elsewhere in the Pacific. Such an element is strong in many Polynesian cases as are Christian elements, since many cults here occurred after extensive missionizing had taken place. Cults in this region were often hostile both to missions and to Europeans who had seized their lands and generated deprivations among potential followers. An excellent case in point is from New Zealand among the Maori people. It is called the Pai Marire ("good and peaceful") or Hau Hau ("life/wind") cult. It was founded by the prophet Te-Ua in 1862 primarily in response to loss of land to the British.

Te-Ua may have been a native priest and had apparently once fought against settlers. He had been a convert to Christianity but was given to trances and other unusual behaviors. He seems to have made claims as to having magically drawn a ship to the coast where there had been a wreck and salvaged cargo. Ultimately, he developed a reputation as having a special relation to the supernatural through a number of incidents such as the restoration of his son to health. Eventually, he had a vision from the angel Gabriel (on behalf of God as an amalgam of Jehovah and Tane, a chief pagan deity), who revealed the elements of a new faith to him. The basic message was as follows. The religion of the British is false and thus so are Europeans who should be driven away. The cult leaders have supernatural power to aid in this activity. If members utter the word Hau several times, this will bring victory and also secure the help of angels who are waiting to assist the Maori in his holy war. The dead will also return. Men and women should also increase their own numbers by living promiscuously so as to procreate many children. When the British are gone, supernaturals from heaven would teach the natives all the technology of Europeans and followers would gain great power.

Ritual literally revolved around a mast salvaged from the shipwreck. This was erected on a sacred platform in the village. Symbols of traditional gods were placed on its crosspiece and streamers tied to its top descended towards the ground. At the base was a small railing and Te-Ua stood behind this like a ship's captain. The prophet apparently considered himself as a new Moses and the Maori as the chosen people of God. As such, it was their sacred duty to fight the British. The rites to promote this endeavor were held each day and were especially potent on each tenth day. Followers would assemble in military order and march clockwise around the pole accompanied by the chanting of magical phrases and holding onto the streamers. These lines were thought to be descended by life/wind spirits to give warriors power and protection. This included immunity from bullets like the ghost shirts in the Ghost Dance among Native Americans. The leader would eventually start a song taken up by others and the marchers would gain in speed until some would get dizzy and fall. New converts were made to stare at the pole until dazed and were then picked up and whirled until they became unconscious. This was also like Ghost Dance activities.

As we have seen, militancy was a central feature of this cult. Before battle, special warriors and their weapons were "baptized" with water and in battle all participants raised their right hand as a special signal and shouted "Pai Marire—Hau Hau" for supernatural aid. As is often the case with fanatics, some initial success in fighting did occur with surprise attacks on isolated British groups. Followers began to join the cult in increasing numbers. Eventually, however, the British organized to put the movement down and after a series of defeats in 1866 the prophet surrendered in exchange for clemency for cult members. This cult did linger on until 1892, at which time it was supplanted by a non-militant, christianized version called Ringatu ("raised hands"), reflecting in name and practice an homage to God. This altered cult, founded by a new prophet, Te Kooti Rikirangi, still has a small following at the present time.

It is instructive to look at another set of examples prior to leaving the Pacific area. These come from Japan and are important for three comparative reasons. First, they developed within the context of a more complex society (although many were begun by rural peasant types). Second, they are being continued at present with large numbers of followers so they represent cult successes. Finally, many are spreading to the United States at the present time. In fact, some scholars consider them to be the cult wave of the future! In Japan, such movements go back a considerable period of time. Neil McFarland believes that recurring crises and problems in Japanese history over the last few hundred years have spawned the deprivations seeding many such new religions. He divides cult developments into five major periods beginning with peasant uprisings in the middle 1800s and concluding with the post World War Two period of occupation after defeat. Hundreds of cults fit into this timetable, many surviving with changes throughout this period. We can briefly examine three examples.

One of the most interesting of these new religions is called the Religion of Heavenly Wisdom, Tenriko. This faith was founded by a farmer's wife, Miki Nakayama, in 1838, at the age of forty. Her son had fallen ill and she had resorted to calling in a traditional healer. She took the place of his usual assistant and in the process she had a trance experience in which she believed she was possessed by a deity. This was the usual practice for revealing the nature of illness, but in this case the deity was "the true and original God," Oyagami. Its message to her was that it would use her body as a shrine. The world could be saved through her body since she would literally be God in an earthly manifestation. Soon afterward her reputation became that of a god-possessed healer and began her religion, in Wilson's terms, as a thaumaturgical cult.

She composed a rather crude series of writings called "the tip of the writing brush" and taught songs and dances as ritual behaviors. She faced a good deal of government pressure due to the non-orthodoxy of her teachings. She died at ninety and was succeeded by a man called Iburi Izo. He also claimed divine inspiration and created a much clearer and refined set of writings. Tenriko also gained a recognized place within the Shinto religion at this point and a main shrine was built to its founder. By 1974 the faith claimed some three million followers. It began to spread to the United States in 1927 and has several thousand members at present, mainly second- and third-generation Japanese. What are its teachings and practices?

The major intellectual foundation of this cult is a belief in Oyagami ("parent deity"). This god is both male and female and is personified as the sun and moon. Further, this god represents heavenly wisdom and the universe as a whole which is its "body." This body unites all opposites. Humans were created by Oyagami as its children. We are given bodies so that we may have an opportunity for joy and happiness and our souls apparently reincarnate into new bodies which represent the future. Unlike some new religions and many orthodox Eastern faiths, there is no final absorption into God. The notion that we are entitled to a joyous, happy life is surely an attractive aspect to this cult.

There is the further notion that since God created us, we are its children (God, the parent deity) and this likewise makes people all brothers and sisters. If we truly wish to live a life of joy, we must treat each other as siblings, doing things that will make other people happy, too. Each person must contribute to the joy of others as part of our responsibility. Beyond this, however, no real formal ethics exists. Drinking, smoking, and secular world involvement are permitted activities. Merely be happy and aid others in their similar quest! Unfortunately, humans have become ignorant of their origins and responsibilities and of the fact that our present body is merely the vehicle for joy. Our minds have become clouded by dust say members of Tenriko and this is reflected in the problems of poverty, sickness, and the like that we witness in the world today. In fact, our bodies actually also serve as a vehicle for God to warn us about our ignorance of these things. If we cleanse our mind and understand the truth about things, these problems will disappear. Not only this, but when all people have come to realize the cult teachings, people will live 115 years in each life incarnation!

One joins this cult by attending a local organization (church). After a time one must go to the national shrine headquarters in Japan and experience training sessions lasting three months. You are then qualified to be a missionary—Yoboku. One can also learn the Ozazuku. This is a special healing prayer employing hand gestures followed by stroking the body of the patient. This harkens back to the healing origins of the movement. Most of the time, however, one engages in regular ritual activities on one Sunday afternoon a month. These take place in a special room before cabinets which act as shrines. There are a number of these. One is for Oyagami, one is used for honoring the founder who still exists on the spirit level, others are for recognizing departed cult members.

Much of the unelaborate rites are Shinto-like, with hand clapping and presenting green branches to gain attention of spirits and for purity. Prayers are given for world salvation and related elements. The most important ritual aspects are dances which reflect the life of joy and other basic cult beliefs. These dances, which are rehearsed so that they represent perfection, are accompanied by hand movements and by songs composed originally by Miki Nakayama. The most important of these which states the desire of God to reveal the truth to the founder is also recited twice a day for general religious merit. Such worship sessions are as entertaining as they are spiritually useful. This, along with the lack of a heavy ethical or withdrawal aspect and the simple message of joy, makes Tenriko an undemanding variety of cult experience.

Another Japanese cult is Seicho-No-Ie, The House of Growth, which was founded by Taniguchi Masaharu. This leader had experienced a rather unhappy early life and had experimented with a number of different cults and religious teachings. He ultimately gained the notion that illness and misfortune are more the creation of one's mind than anything else and that to change one's life for the better, one could utilize the power of the mind; the "wish becoming the father of the reality." Around 1930 he received a divine relevation concerning this and that, in fact, the material world around us does not exist as such but is a mere manifestation of our minds.

This prophet then began a series of writings and gained followers. His religion was repressed after World War Two due to his overt support for that conflict. He then changed his teachings somewhat (here is the adaptation phase of cult growth) claiming that they really represented the truth behind all religions. His own group he said was not really a religious organization. In fact, this leader supposedly depends upon a special intuition allowing him to identify the real truths in the writings and beliefs of all religions, especially Buddhism and Christianity. Like Tenriko, this is a successful modern movement claiming three million followers worldwide. These individuals do not have to relinquish their ties to their original faiths. Seicho-No-Ie will only make one's older religion better! There are close to 10,000 members in the United States.

As in the case of Tenriko and many other Japanese expressions, this cult promises not only to overcome illness but also other human problems. It teaches that we are originally pure beings because we are created by the deity (seen as Buddha or God). The world around us is also pure and free from any problems or unhappiness since it is a manifestation of our mind. Unfortunately, wrong thinking can cause bad conditions such as illness. Such thinking then becomes self-fulfilling because the more we think wrongly, the worse things become. "The fear of the disease makes the disease more fearful." To correct this situation and create human happiness we must correct our ways of thought since it is our mind which creates these conditions; you become what you think!

Right thinking includes the notion that as a child of God we are perfect. This should give one inner peace and aid in the development of a proper state of mind. One should also accept things as good and show one's gratitude; repeating in mantra-like fashion the phrase Arigato

Gozaimasu: "Thank you very much." The follower's good mental condition will then affect the environment which is its reflection. Such teachings are given by headquarters in Tokyo, mostly in written forms, and reach down to local groups. Such local organizations are called Mutual Love Societies and meet each day in the early morning for meditation. This aids followers to realize a oneness with God and to purify the mind. Lecture and testimonies also occur as do monthly meetings for the same purposes in members' houses. Aside from aiding in the mental creation of conditions of happiness and perfection, this cult also claims to reconstruct the original truth of religion and in a more secularized sense to seek the solutions to some of the more immediate problems faced by the Japanese after their last war. This involves a very nationalistic and overtly political set of goals such as teaching traditional history, revising the constitution, and the like. In this sense, Seicho-No-Ie fits with some of the more activist new Japanese religions.

We can examine a last cult from among the variety of new religious movements in Japan. This one is called Perfect Liberty Order and was begun (with a different name) by Tokumitsu Kanada around 1912. This man had been attracted to mystical things in general and to Shingon Buddhism whose priests often underwent ordeals in the mountains in their search for mystical insights. He himself did likewise and eventually, as in the case of many cult founders in this area, began to cure the sick by absorption of their illnesses into himself. He gained followers and began to systematize a new faith by listing principles of belief and practice. To him, Buddhist and Shinto deities were all aspects of a single overarching God, and humans were also manifestations of this "parent deity" and so were all equal in brotherhood.

In 1916 his cult was joined by an ex-Zen monk Tokuharu and his son Tokuchika. Kanada died soon after, but he said that if a tree were planted at the site of his death a person would appear and add three new principles of belief. Such a person was to be the next leader of the faith. Tokuharu did so, meditated for five years, and in mystical visions the three principles were revealed to him. This justified his position as the new leader of the cult. At this point the religion was called the Way of Man, but it met with much governmental opposition. Tokuchika succeeded his father as leader, only to be placed in jail and the cult basically disbanded. After World War Two he was released and the cult began anew with fresh revelation of its principles. It was renamed Perfect Liberty; a Japanese cult with an English name! The cult spread rapidly and today there are more than two million followers worldwide and over five thousand in the United States. Its headquarters and chief temple is near Osaka. What are its beliefs and practices?

There are twenty-one basic beliefs or principles in this cult. These include statements such as the following. "Life is art." "The whole life of the individual is a continuous succession of self-expressions." "The individual is a manifestation of God." "We suffer if we do not manifest ourself." "Live in perfect liberty." What do these statements mean? Life is art is the real catch phrase of the movement. A person is the result of his or her whole pattern of life. Our job, family relations, hobbies, whatever, should be unified together into perfect harmony; into what we might call a single life-style. This must be integrated together the way "an artist paints a picture." Such will become a true work of art if we also express ourselves perfectly in our life, inasmuch as we are a manifestation of God. We can be happy if we can express that which we are as well as our own uniqueness, our true self or personality. If we can do this, we are true artists who live in perfect liberty and like an artist we can bring out the potential of some medium: ourselves! We will know happiness and be satisfied if we have done our best work in these respects.

Such a life-style reflects the natural order of things. If we forget this, if we are ego centered, if we forget to include the welfare of humans as we paint the canvas of our lives, this will be displeasing to God, Mioyaokami, and we will suffer the consequences. Suffering is in fact a communication from God: a *Misirase,* or "divine warning." Here, practice intersects with belief. Specific reasons for suffering are not revealed by God except through the intermediating efforts of the leader of the cult or other special persons called "parents." The suffering cult member must either see them directly or fill out a special form and send it to them. They then identify the specifics of the cause of the suffering and suggest what can be done to relieve it. The leader Tokuchika, like the founder Kanada, can also in principle take the suffering of followers onto his own shoulders.

One need not wait for suffering to be motivated into ritual action. In addition to the use of a special hand gesture on various occasions there is an early morning daily worship service at the headquarters and at larger churches throughout the world. At this time a special hymn is sung followed by a formal prayer of commitment which identifies the follower with Mioyaokami. Other formal prayers follow along with testimonies as to the artistic successes in life. A sermon is followed by a breakfast to enhance fellowship. A general thanksgiving rite occurs on the twenty-first day of the month. The form taken by this at the international headquarters is most elaborate and is highlighted by the leader renewing his vows to take on the suffering of his followers. There is also an annual founder's day rite in August (for Tokuharu, not Kanada) replete with extensive fireworks and prayers for world peace. Japanese cults such as Perfect Liberty and the others briefly characterized in this chapter predictably will spread in American society in the near future. They make only a few ritual and other demands on converts and touch the nerve of self-interest and perfectability. We can now briefly characterize a few African examples for comparative purposes.

There are a great number of African religious movements. This is not surprising given the size of this geographical region and the long and often unpleasant colonial history. There are in fact so many cults that they come close to defying attempts at classification. Many, certainly, are best understood against the activities of Christian missionizing, since these individuals were often responsible for making the native African peoples aware of their lesser status with respect to Europeans. Islamic missionaries surely played a role in cult formation as well. Rather than attempting to cover all varieties of cults from the African experience or put them precisely into categories suggested previously, we can simply follow James W. Fernandez and suggest four main tendencies that apply to most cults. Some of these movements are essentially Christian but have separated somewhat in the attempt to coordinate membership and improve status. Others at least partially reject Christian religious aspects and seek more traditional and more immediate solutions to the problems of life. Still other cults attempt to merge Christian elements with the past and there are types which are prophetic and assume the coming of some kind of golden age. Fernandez calls these cults Separatist, Nativist, Reformative, and Messianic, but we can detect the applicability of other terms of classification to them. At any rate, we can conclude this chapter with three brief illustrations of what are contemporary movements.

One of the most interesting of these new religions is called the Jamaa movement. Jamaa means "family." This religion was begun prior to 1960 by a Franciscan missionary originally from Belgium who had come to Katanga. This man, Placide Tempels, had arrived in Africa as a typical Christian missionary in support of colonialism. After a time he came to feel that his own ideas and Christianity per se did not fit well in the context of native culture. Early on, he became impressed with the thought of African Bantu tribes. This interest culminated in a book on their philosophy. He eventually came to question not only the idea of colonialism but sought to promote respect for the native culture, considering the peoples themselves as equals rather than "helpless children." In particular, he hoped to enlighten them on the viability of their own culture and adapt Christianity to it; to recast the missionary gospel in native terms! He also stressed heavy personal involvement as the way in which this might be done.

In 1953, Tempels was appointed pastor at a mining settlement near Kolowezi in Katanga and began to initiate activity along the above lines. His message found a good response due to the emerging self-awareness and desire for liberation of the people involved. These miners were dissatisfied, lacked hope, and felt inferior to Europeans. The Jamaa doctrine, however, held out the idea of human dignity, or *Umuntu* ("being man"). The cult spread rapidly after 1960 due to the independence of the Congo and the succession of Katanga, although Tempels himself left Africa for health reasons in 1962.

The basic pattern of organization of this movement is for a leader to attract followers (originally Tempels, later disciples) who develop their own followers as they are trained in the doctrine. Recruits are married couples and already Christians. What seems to be a lack of many distinct rituals is thus explained. Jamaa is basically grafted onto Christian doctrine and practices as a special addition. A Jamaa group is definable due to its engagement in certain other activities based on extra beliefs. Basically, three types of such activities occur. The first is a weekly meeting, the Mafundisho, which involves an introductory prayer and hymn, instruction in doctrine by leaders and other acts. Second is the Pulan, an intergroup meeting that includes the presentation of candidates for "degrees" of membership. The last rite, Ku-ingisha, is performed by a priest who (like Tempels) is a member of the movement. This rite involves some revelation of secrets, examination of candidates' knowledge, prophesy, and practical directions relative to the initiatory experiences that occur at this time.

To become a fully initiated member, the married couple must go through at least three years of instruction—some public though mostly on a private basis. It also requires that secrecy be maintained concerning the doctrine. There are three degrees or "ways" that must be achieved. Each degree is actualized in the Ku-ingisha ritual depending on the level the candidates have already attained. In the first degree, the candidates obtain the thought of *life/force*, or *Uzima*. They receive a consciousness of their vocation by uniting themselves with Jesus Christ and the Virgin Mary. They pray and meditate and purportedly have a dream experience of such union. They become "born again." In the second degree the candidates receive the notion of *union in love*. This is to say union between husband and wife. Prayer and meditation are again involved and the ritual experience consists of ritual intercourse between the husband and wife. At this point the marriage is elevated to the Jamaa level for group unity as well.

In the third degree or way, the couple acquire the knowledge of *Uzazi*, or *fertility/fecundity*. A dramatic activity occurs between the priest and the candidates in which God's descent on the Holy Family is re-enacted; the priest becoming the Christ child to the candidate's Mary and Joseph. Having given birth to Jesus the couple are now full-fledged members and have the right to introduce other people into the movement. They have acquired parenthood and their fertility will expand cult membership. Thus is hope and identity given followers who become very special kinds of Christians.

The Bwiti cult among the Fang peoples of Northern Gabon is another example of a new African religion. As elsewhere in Africa, cultural changes (especially in the economic realm) among these peoples have caused uncertainty, and the loss of older religious traditions have paved the way for new supernatural solutions. This cult began around 1900 and was originally an attempt at perpetuating an older religious activity through the borrowing of new traits from other peoples. Such new aspects in what was essentially ancestor ritual was viewed as being more effective in the contacting of such powers which had been seen as growing increasingly distant because of Christian influences. As this religious movement grew, it divided into a number of divisions or subcults and the following brief description pertains only to one of these: The Asumege Ening ("beginning of life"). This name suggests the kind of revitalization we have previously discussed and represents in the awareness of members the desire to rebuild their culture along more satisfying lines and to give members a sense of unity and solidarity. This they refer to as Nlem-Mvore—"One-Heartedness."

Rituals in this cult revolve around special cult houses where, as in the Peyote cult, members engage in all-night activities. Rites begin at six in the evening and end at six in the morning. Dancing comprises a major activity, but ritual acts are not continuous. Prayers are offered to God and the ancestors and an intoxicant is employed to aid in spiritual contact. The ecstatic state thus gained, "leaving oneself" is not seen as possession in the Caribbean sense, however, since such spirits apparently do not come into the person; worshippers have to leave themselves to visit them.

The actual ritual occurs in two main phases. From its inception until about midnight the assembled members engage in dancing which depicts the creation of the world and humans along with other Christian motifs. Members differ in their appreciation and knowledge of the symbolic content of these performances, but most do recognize a theme of birth and creation. After midnight the theme of the dances changes to death and destruction. The actual symbolic content represents a mixture of native and Christian themes such as Fang migrations and the expulsion of Adam and Eve from the Garden.

The highest ritual endeavors occur between cycles of dances. Cult followers re-establish union with the ancestral spirits. These have come at this point near to the cult house from the deeper forest and the opportunity has arisen for the living and the dead to gain the one-heartedness mentioned previously. In effect, the living-dead distinction can be overcome, as can life's problems. To accomplish this state of affairs, the members line up in a column and each lights a torch. They then file out of the cult house, go through the village, and out into the forest along a series of paths. This movement lures the ancestors to follow the living back to the cult house and perhaps attracts those which have not yet responded to the dancing and earlier activities. When members return, the column turns inward into increasingly tighter circles until all marchers have formed a solid group and their upraised torches have become a single flame. At this point the living members and the ancestors have become one in unity. This "peak experience" at least temporarily allows members to overcome their uncertainty and deprivations. Certainly such good feelings are a fine inducement for the continuation of the rites, such acts becoming somewhat (as in the case of much in religion) an end in themselves. We can now examine a final African cult example.

The Tigari cult has spread along parts of the Guinea Coast of West Africa among Akan peoples such as the Fanti. It began about twenty-five years ago and derives its name from the worship of a deity (or supernatural force) called Tigari. While this cult has value in its activities along the lines of Bwiti, it has a strong thaumaturgical element for giving relief to medical and other problems. These include such things as getting jobs, protection when traveling, and doing well at school. It can also supply protection against evil magic which is thought to be on the rise due to European influences and deprivations. In these respects, it is much like the Convince cult and others dealt with in the previous chapter.

The leaders (priests) of the Tigari cult are males but otherwise have no special qualities. This makes them different from traditional manipulators of the supernatural who were possessed by spirits and endured a long and complicated apprenticeship. These new leaders train for only a few months. They learn how to address the deity and how to do the relevant ritual actions. Such training is costly, but often people in a local area will sponsor someone to train and so make available the supposed benefits to themselves. Ritual activities are held over a three-day period and occur about every six weeks. Dancing, drumming, praying, and food offerings are involved. Again, except for the lack of possession, activities are very similar to Caribbean expressions. Like many cults we have examined there is also a formal ethics that members are enjoined to follow. This is comprised of seventeen rules of a "thou shalt not" nature. These include not lying, gossiping, stealing, adultering, practicing evil magic, or challenging the power of Tigari. If a cult member fails to follow such injunctions, he will suffer illness, bad luck, or death at the hands of Tigari.

To become a member one merely goes to the local leader. That person recites the rules and pays a membership fee. The new member eats a kola nut specially blessed by the priest. One then attends the periodic rites and has the additional privilege of making special requests for help as needed. One goes to a cult shrine, or Bombaa, for this function. This is in a compound in which there is a special cement on a clay bench with a hole in it. The person with the difficulty states this to the priest and pays a fee. The priest then taps a kola nut (sacred object) on the bench and states the devotee's problem/request to Tigari (for that job or protection from bad magic, etc.). The devotee then eats the kola nut and promises a further offering to the deity if the request is granted. Often, in these cases money is given to the priest rather than the traditional chicken or other animal. If successful, such activities reinforce the power and benefit of this cult in the minds of both adherents and potential cult members. These cults, Jamaa, Mwiti, and Tigari, are but a small sample of new African religions. We can now return to more theoretical issues relevant to the cult experience.

Chapter 9

THE WORLD OF THE CULTS

In the previous chapters of this book, we have examined a great many cults both in the United States and elsewhere in space and time. We have cast some light on the careers of these new religions and how they develop and have dealt with some of the aspects which are involved in the conversion of individuals to such organizations. We have examined who joins and why they do so, as well as some of the attempts by scholars to classify cults. We noted that there is not a great amount of agreement on some of these topics, for example, on classification, whereas on other topics, such as why people join, some communalities do occur. This book has only scratched the surface on all of these topics and the serious reader will want to consult the Bibliographic Essays at the end of this book and then go beyond them.

This is not the place to attempt a reconsideration of all of the differences relating to the study of cults. Such would require a long book in itself and the intention of the present volume is merely to introduce some of the aspects of the cult experience. However, we can bring up three points of interest. First, is there any consensus we can draw as to what cults are? We left this question unanswered back in Chapter 1 and some closure on the topic would be valuable. Second, it seems reasonable to ask why cults in this country seemed to flourish so much in the sixties and seventies, and there is a major body of literature on this topic that we can briefly sample. Finally, it remains to ask if cults (at least in this country) are valid forms of religious experience. Are they to be feared for their excesses? Are they bogus faiths? Or are they valuable mechanisms that are beneficial to their memberships? Again, we can select a few samples of scholarly work on this important topic.

There are a great many definitions of cults. Partially, this is a reflection of scholarly differences between sociologists who study such phenomena in our own society and anthropologists who seek such expressions among tribal peoples. But even within such fields of scholarship differences of opinion are extraordinarily large. We did some listing of traits in Chapter 1, but such lists are uneven. Some say, for example, that cults are authoritarian in structure, others that they lack structure. Other traits are agreed upon, such as rigidity of thought, but this hardly separates them from traditional religious (and other) organizations. Like sects, they tend to reject the world, but unlike them they are said not to derive from orthodoxy; they are new religions not connected to traditional churches. And, of course, they can be defined from the perspective of their functions. They cater to a need for belonging and many other things and this adds still more confusion. So what are cults?

As mentioned above this is scarcely the place to attempt to resolve this issue if such is possible, but we can perhaps indulge a few comments. It does appear that cults we have examined all share the trait of having been founded by a leader (or leaders) possessing great personal charisma. These are people who get the organization underway due to their energy and attractiveness. Handsome Lake, Smohalla, L. Ron Hubbard, and Meher Baba are examples of such individuals. Part of the charm of such persons is that they claim to have had special supernatural experiences, or at least supernatural knowledge, and to be able to make that available to those who become their followers. This supernatural aspect may be to obtain the level of operating thetan, join with Krsna, overcome Europeans, relieve illness, or merely to get a better job. Ecstatic aspects may or may not be involved.

Such groups in purest form are small and, except internally, limited in influence. They have not grown and developed into a secure, accepted niche within the wider context of their occurrence; for example, within the United States at present or in some colonial area. Once such religions do grow in numbers and general acceptance (not necessarily dominance), they have most likely become some other species of religious phenomena! This means that some of the Japanese-inspired cults in America today have lost that status in their homeland.

Members join such groups voluntarily, sometimes with a formal conversion procedure and experience, sometimes not. People join cults because they are dissatisfied with themselves or with the world around them. They may be experiencing personal problems of one sort or the other, or with society in general. Such difficulties may be caused by the social milieu itself—America today—or the intrusion of outside people and societies as is so often the case in tribal cult configurations.

Finally, such groups espouse new religious beliefs and behaviors. Such may be outside the realm of traditional orthodoxy or they may be partly inspired by it. The syncretistic and eclectic nature of cults has previously been commented upon. In all of these terms, then, it seems as though cults, both in our own and other societies, might be characterized along the following lines: *Cults are small, new, innovative, and marginal religious groups based on a charismatic founder/leader who, based on some special supernatural knowledge and/or experience, is capable of helping followers deal with their individual and/or societal dissatisfactions.* This definition may help the reader remember the groups we have discussed in this book and to recognize similar phenomena. In these respects cults in this society and among tribal peoples are very similar.

It is worthwhile taking a bit of time to involve ourselves in one of the interesting and controversial topics with respect to cults in this country. This is often referred to as the notion of consciousness reformation and it purports to explain the great rise of new religions in the 1960s. There was the development of a large number of new cults at this time, both foreign and domestic, although other periods in American history have seen such florescence. The media attention given to them may also have somewhat obscured their importance and membership numbers. Nonetheless, we can examine what many scholars feel was a key element behind the rise of these cults. This was, they say, nothing less than a basic change in the way youth were thinking in terms of how they viewed the world. Such views can be called modes of consciousness or styles of moral meaning, and in the 1960s a number of things occurred to lead to a shift in such thinking that paved the way for the rise of many cults.

We can start with the work of Robert W. Bellah here, a scholar whose name is closely associated with the concept of consciousness reformation. In his view there was a "conjunction or dissatisfaction" especially on the part of young people. These included protests both by Blacks and women, a sense that social problems were not being met, and Vietnam as a kind of catalyst. The result was a disaffection from the common understandings of American culture and a questioning of the legitimacy of American institutions. Where had past meanings come from? Bellah suggests that the American consciousness had somewhat imperfectly grafted two styles of meaning together: biblical religion and utilitarian individualism. The latter had finally overcome the former by the sixties. Other scholars believe more than two modes of consciousness existed and were in conflict. Among these are Charles Y. Glock, Robert Wuthnow, and

Steven M. Tipton. We can somewhat put their views together to get a handle on this situation.

Biblical religion or what is also called theism, or the revealed style, is the oldest influence on American values and ways of thinking. It is an authoritative style and holds that the principal agent of control in life is God, who is the ultimate arbiter of destiny. This view has little real regard for human achievement in the individual sense, since this is ultimately God's doing. God is the agent who governs life and we should do what God commands. An act is good if we obey this authority. A human is good if we follow God. As Bellah has put it, this view ultimately was taken to be a kind of national view, with America as the new Israel with its citizens having the "freedom" to follow such correct behaviors; a nation under God as it were.

A second and more modern view that all the above authors seem to agree upon is that of utilitarian individualism. This view supposes that humans are in control of what happens to themselves and leads, consequently, to a higher regard for human achievement and to a more consequential style of life. This view developed with industrialism and involves the individual maximizing his or her own self-interest with less a sense of being a part of God's community. Here, the question is not of God's will but of what I want and my happiness. Right activity is that which produces this consequence. A person is good if he or she is happy, if they satisfy their desires. This is certainly a this-worldly rather than an other-worldly perspective, with the means to money, power, and other desired ends held to be most important.

These two views had coexisted, but by the 1960s the latter had come to dominate. At this time there were also the problems alluded to previously which helped to bring these views and their contradictions into relief. According to many scholars the "counterculture" began to reject individualistic utilitarianism and the biblical view. In this last case this occurred either because individualism had already destroyed it or because the two views had reached such an accommodation that to reject either was to reject both! The reader should refer back to Stark and Bainbridge for information on the secularization of mainline American religion. A new consciousness began to emerge that "said" that the "continuous expansion of wealth and power," to use Bellah's terms, was not enough on which to base the quality of one's life. What about personal feelings, inner experience, and social relations? With all the current problems in America, what about a more humane society? Tipton sees such a view as ultimately derived from a style of moral meaning he calls the romantic tradition. This view holds that the individual is "not an agent pursuing self-interest, but an experiencing and expressing personality."

It must also be mentioned that another view was probably very important in shaping the challenge to the status quo. This was the view from science, especially the social sciences, which both Glock and Wuthnow see as very important. This view is that life is not governed by God or the free actions of individuals but by social and other forces. Human destiny is not in our own hands entirely or in those of God! Remember, many cult members are educated middle-class youth whose past experiences best situate them to be aware of an act upon such knowledge. Unfortunately, the sixties counterculture could agree on the necessity of change and on rejecting biblical and individual styles of consciousness, but they apparently could not agree on how this could be done best. Values from older views were rejected and science does not concern itself with values in this way. It says what is, but not morally what should be! It could not provide a new form of moral meaning. Existing, then, in a moral vacuum American youth began turning to other forms which could provide meaning and authority; to alternative religions with their (often Asian) emphasis on inner experience, harmony with nature, and intense relations to gurus. This general view is, in consciousness reformation terms, what Wuthnow calls mysticism; that the meaning of life and its governing forms cannot be understood by human intellect. This is certainly a view characteristic of many cults. It is a view very much in keeping with the new feelings of the sixties.

This model of cultural transformation simply says that the traditional and modern views (forms of consciousness) were both called into question by science and the various dissatisfactions of the sixties. This occurred regardless of whether they were in conflict with one another or not, and a new view based on personal feelings emerged that sought new outlets. Cults supplied these outlets. At the same time, cults represented in styles of moral meaning the emergence of a new consciousness. Do we have any real evidence of such a mental change?

In his study on the consciousness reformation, Robert Wuthnow sampled San Francisco residents relative to their allegiance to theism, individualism, science, and mystical views and believed that his data showed differences in willingness to experiment with new behaviors. Those embracing theism, the older consciousness, scored low on change, and "mystics" seemed most open to experimentation with new life-styles.

This seemingly indicates the need for a shift in each orientation prior to cult involvement and other experimentation. Bainbridge and Stark, however, did an approximately similar study and came to believe that the questions used in the study for people to respond to only revealed a real meaning system in the case of theism. The questions used in Wuthnow to construct the individualism category, for example, are unrelated to each other and not shared. Moreover, it is the conclusion of these authors that the categories other than theism do not show consistent effects in behavioral terms, either. So for Bainbridge and Stark, the other meaning systems do not appear to explain attitudes and behavior patterns and may not really exist. They believe that many of the effects determined by Wuthnow are really produced by the older theistic meaning system.

These authors also state the proposition that individuals will only have benefit from such consciousness structures if they are connected by social relations to an organization that embraces such a view. Wuthnow's study was largely attitudinal rather than behavioral; an examination of individual belief systems. Certainly, theism has a long group tradition behind it. One can wonder about the other styles of meaning in this respect. One study has, however, added some credence to Wuthnow's original work. In a study of urban communes—that is to say, groups of believers as well as behavior—Angela Aidala has demonstrated that only a small percentage of members were oriented towards a traditional theistic view of reality. Most expressed a "modern" perspective, especially the mystical orientation. Considering this was the high experimentation category for Wuthnow's study and that collectively and behaviorally these people are experimenters in communes, this looks like good evidence (if limited) that consciousness shifts and new forms of behavior, including religious experimentation, are intimately connected.

If there are problems in defining what a cult is in definitional terms and in specifying the precise conditions under which they are formed, how much greater is the difficulty of evaluating their legitimacy and performance in American (or any other) society? This difficulty goes beyond the fact of their new religion or non-traditional status. Some of those discussed were desire for community and friendship, desire for engagement and solving problems—personal or societal, desire for independence and direction, the desire for a special experience of ecstasy—that personal encounter with the supernatural, the alienation and/or rejection of modern culture motive, and the seeker/searcher inducement relative to personal growth. Cults do seem to meet deprivational and other needs. Are cults, then, not valuable social phenomena? Do they not play a useful and significant role in society? My general impression from a serious survey of the literature is that the answers to these questions by most social scientists is at least a qualified yes. Cults may have excesses and occasionally one may seem to be very wrongly guided as in the case of Jim Jones and the People's Temple movement, but on the whole the help they provide for their converts seems to be viewed in positive terms.

How much of such a conclusion is to be considered a by-product of a functionalist social science approach, one that looks for the contributions made by specific societal structures and behaviors, is difficult to assess. Likewise, the seemingly lukewarm endorsement of many cults may be an unconscious reflection of the value-free perspective of science in general, which describes but does not take sides in evaluation. Perspectives by non-scientists, primarily family and friends, seems more heavily negative on the subject of cults as do representatives of mainline faiths and the occasional governmental official. In the case of many families, the very real anxiety, confusion, helplessness, and the like, obviously prompt an overreaction in many cases and resort to the brainwashing explanations discussed previously; allegations perhaps dismissed too easily by scientists! Families may overemphasize the negative aspects as much as some scholars accentuate the positive. Can such differences of opinion be reconciled? Certainly this has not occurred in any literature to date that I am aware of. Moreover, such an analysis is not generally applied to traditional religions either, which surely handicaps evaluation of non-traditional types.

We can, however, out of obvious reader interest in this topic, give some examples of moves in the direction of possible evaluation of cults. One approach is to list certain cult characteristics and maintain that if these occur highly clustered together or if any of them are taken to excess, then the cult so involved is probably bogus and harmful with respect to fulfilling the very real needs of its members. We can use as an example of this approach an article by Susan Anderson. It should be stated that she basically uses these characters to define a cult (if enough such characters occur it is a cult), but we can manipulate her criteria along good-bad dimensions.

She sees cults as having high degrees of control over individual freedom—activities, associations and life decisions—especially through their capacities for psychological coercion and deception. For our purposes we can suppose that if the specifics of either of these is high, the disfunctions of cult membership may outweigh the advantages. We have certainly met up with aspects of these characters before, but descriptively and in the chapter on conversion. Now we are examining them in evaluative terms. What would indicate that a cult is guilty of a high degree of psychological coercion? Anderson characterizes this feature in ten ways.

We can represent these in list format:

1) Isolation of members from past and external sources of social support. This includes a lack of privacy for cult members, the exclusive interaction with other cult members and being cut off from family and friends.

2) Giving love and support to members only on the condition that they express the beliefs of the cult, the "party line."

3) A lack of tolerance for any diversity of opinion.

4) At least the threat of physical harm in the event of disobedience to cult beliefs and routines. This may be coupled with:

5) The threat of spiritual/mystical punishment. Here a person may be threatened with lack of salvation or supernatural punishment if they fail to conform. This is more common than physical types.

6) The eliciting of confessions and personal life history. This gives the cult insight into what makes a person vulnerable and easier to manipulate.

7) The induction of psychological stress in converts so they come to feel guilty about how they used to think or when they still think about non-cult matters.

8) Dividing the world up into the cult which is good and outsiders who are evil and less than fully human.

9) Continual verbal and sensory pounding of the member/convert with cult propaganda.

10) The deprivation of sleep, food, or whatever so the members are more passive and thus easier to control.

If a cult scores high on these points it would not offer valuable experiences to members. Deception can also be overdone in cults according to Anderson and this takes the following forms:

1) The lying about the purpose of the cult to new or potential converts.

2) The dissemination of inaccurate information to the outside world (family, media, etc.).

3) Not making converts fully aware of the future changes they will have to make after joining the group.

4) Emphasizing that only one authority exists for decisions.

5) Leaders "hoodwinking" members into believing that they behave in all ways just like members: abstain from sex, live in poverty or whatever.

6) Limiting alternatives for behavior and omitting other legitimate options if they run counter to cult goals.

It could be argued, recall the discussion of the work of Rosabeth Kanter, that any organization in its effort to maximize conversion opportunities and procedures will have to display many of these characters or fail! It could also be argued, however, that the more of these characters a given cult displays and the higher the degree to which each is an endorsed (or even unconscious) practice, the more limited will be its value for the convert or member. In very high degrees it could be maintained that substantial damage will be done to the persons involved. So we can evaluate any cult expression along these lines. However, while the student of religious behavior can do this, we must remember that the religious seeker is not likely to pre-evaluate groups which may capture his or her interest. The supermarket of cults does not advertise its "prices" up front, only when the convert "checks out"!

This approach which lists potential bad cult characters also has another limitation, one perhaps even more difficult to grapple with in a scientific fashion. This is the truth of the beliefs themselves, a subject seldom taken on in the literature of new religions, and for that matter, older ones either. Can some cults be demonstrated to more accurately represent reality than others? Is the belief in operating thetans less valid than the existence of Krsna or parent deity? Science would find it difficult to objectively compare such claims. Yet, some writers have suggested a way around this, a way to use criteria as we have previously discussed and evaluate the genuineness of cults without bringing specific beliefs under analysis. This is an approach primarily forwarded from the area of transpersonal psychology.

Scholarly writing from this perspective takes the assumption implicitly or explicitly that humans are capable of reaching some type of higher level of consciousness, of transcending what we normally think of as human life. Many such writers characterize this as the need to surrender to something higher than ourselves. In this sense spiritual and other groups can be evaluated in terms of how well they meet this goal. Francis Vaughan, for example, assumes we can evaluate such groups in terms of their legitimacy; how well they meet the psychological needs of members, and their authority, the degree to which they do facilitate transcendence. In concrete terms, such groups should "empower members to accept love, to appreciate unity and diversity, to be capable of detachment and self-transcendence." They should also have leaders who do not use their special charisma to manipulate their followers and the groups should not isolate itself physically or psychologically from the outside world. If a cult accomplishes these things, it is valuable rather than harmful. There is clear overlap here to Anderson's list, even though the basic framework on which evaluation is based is different.

Another writer representing this perspective is John Welwood, who speaks of the pathology of some spiritual groups. Bogus groups in these terms are those in which the leader controls the follower by playing on his or her sense of personal inadequacy and lack of self-worth. A true "master" is one who has deep respect for human dignity, who encourages self-respect rather than attempting to undermine it. Second, bogus groups have an ideology that is closed in the sense that no questioning or deviation is permitted, an "airtight world view" in his terms. The leader with this knowledge gives the follower the word about the way things are! Acceptable groups and gurus allow for ambiguity and paradox in doctrine and allow for questions. Leaders share their wisdom in an experimental way (this is how I see it) rather than by passing on exact truth. Doubt is not sin in such groups. Thirdly, bogus groups keep members in line by manipulating the hopes and fears of members. They promise them salvation if they follow directions and threaten them with dire results if they stray from the group. A good leader or group in this sense does not manipulate emotions but appeals to the intelligence of followers to continue in their efforts for self-transcendence; to try to experience some higher type of being.

Bogus spiritual organizations also rely heavily on "group think," keeping members together with no outside thinking, activities, or even contacts. They maintain a strict insider-outsider frame of reference. We have commented on this technique many times before. Welwood believes that an authentic leader or group who recognizes the need for personal privacy to aid in the search for growth and does not cut off members from outside contact is in fact concerned with all people, not just special followers. Finally (and this is a most interesting point seldom commented upon), a true spiritual leader and organization will be based on some kind of tradition and he or she will themself have undergone spiritual training and discipline. Bogus cults have leaders who are often self-styled prophets who have created their teachings by themselves. Of course, this falls short of saying how any new faith may germinate! Welwood's five marks of spiritual pathology are, however, very useful and they match up, even with his assumptions about transcendence that other scholars may not have, with negative comments we have previously discussed.

Other, more ambitious schemes follow these I have just mentioned and are cited in the Bibliographic Essays. The point behind the whole transpersonal perspective is that it is, in Welwood's terms, "healthy to want to go beyond ourselves." If cults are of the non-bogus variety, then they are fully legitimate means by which a person can accomplish such a task. As he also nicely puts it, if we reject all cults because some are bogus it's like refusing to use money because some is counterfeit! Remember our definition of religion in Chapter 1 spoke of the attempt to transform oneself to a higher level of existence. Cults, misguided or otherwise, do, as we have seen, represent such attempts. We can utilize lists such as those supplied by Anderson, Vaughan, Welwood, and others (with or without beliefs in higher levels of being) and evaluate at least the American cults with which we have become a little familiar. This book has attempted to introduce such a possibility to readers and to make them aware in a very introductory fashion of the cult experience.

BIBLIOGRAPHIC ESSAYS

Chapter 1

There are a great many books which deal with religion in a general way. The following might be of most use to readers of the present work. A very readable world survey of past and present faiths is Robert S. Ellwood, Jr., *Many Peoples, Many Faiths* (Englewood Cliffs, Prentice-Hall, 1987). This book also treats the basic forms of religious expression. For tribal religions see my own small text, *Primitive Religion* (Totowa, Littlefield Adams, 1978). This book also has two chapters on general dimensions and definitions of religion. Homing in specifically on religious expressions are the following: Frederick J. Streng, *Understanding The Religious Life* (Belmont, Wadsworth, 1985). This book nicely covers all the various ways of being religious. Illustrating these ways is Frederick S. Streng, Charles L. Lloyd, Jr., and Jay T. Allen, *Ways Of Being Religious* (Englewood Cliffs, Prentice-Hall, 1973). For a discussion of both the experience of religion and elements comprising this phenomenon, there is the still useful work by Winston L. King, *Introduction To Religion* (New York, Harper and Row, 1968). A somewhat controversial model for religious thinking occurs in Mircea Eliade, *The Sacred And The Profane* (New York, Harper and Row, 1959).

The more specific topics of churches and sects are covered in most textbooks on the sociology of religion. For example, see Glynn M. Vernon, *Sociology of Religion* (New York, McGraw-Hill, 1962) and J. Milton Yinger, *The Scientific Study Of Religion* (New York, MacMillan, 1970). See also Bryan R. Wilson, *Religion In Sociological Perspective* (New York, Oxford University Press, 1982). The key distinction in this chapter is from Benton Johnson, "On Church and Sect," in *American Sociological Review, 28:*539–549, 1963.

The general literature on cults is also enormous and contradictory. For modern types the following have been consulted: Willa Appel, *Cults In America* (New York, Holt, Rinehart, and Winston, 1983); Robert S. Ellwood, Jr., *Religious and Spiritual Groups in Modern America* (Englewood

Cliffs, Prentice-Hall, 1973); Irving I. Zaretsky and Mark P. Leone (Eds.), *Religious Movements in America* (Princeton, Princeton University Press, 1974) (especially section 7). See also J. Gordon Melton and Robert L. Moore, *The Cult Experience* (New York, Pilgrim Press, 1982); and J. Gordon Melton, *Encyclopedic Handbook of Cults in America* (New York, Garland, 1986). One of the most recent overall studies is that of Rodney Stark and William Sims Bainbridge, *The Future of Religion* (Berkeley, University of California Press, 1985). This represents the fruition of many years of research and may be the best guide available. It does presuppose a little familiarity with the phenomenon in question. Two very specific articles on cults, among many, are Allan W. Eister, "A Theory of Cults," in *Journal for the Scientific Study of Religion, 11:*319–333, 1972 and Geoffrey K. Nelson, "The Concept of Cult," in *Sociological Review, 16:*351–362, 1968. Most books and articles offer a definition of cults.

Chapter 2

For the Hare Krsna cult I have used the following sources: J. Stilson Judah, *Hare Krishna and the Counter Culture* (New York, John Wiley, 1974) and his article "The Hare Krishna Movement," in Irving I. Zaretsky and Mark P. Leone (Eds.), *Religious Movements in Contemporary America* (Princeton, Princeton University Press, 1975), pp. 463–478. See also Francine Danner, *The American Children of Krsna* (New York, Holt, Rinehart, and Winston, 1976); and Gregory Johnson, "The Hare Krishna in San Francisco," in Charles Y. Glock and Robert N. Bellah (Eds.), *The New Religious Consciousness,* (Berkeley, University of California Press, 1976), pp. 31–51. Two other volumes are of interest here. Steven J. Gelberg (Ed.), *Hare Krishna, Hare Krishna* (New York, Grove Press, 1983) has an interview format and an insider perspective; and E. Burke Rochford, Jr., *Hare Krishna In America* (New Brunswick, Rutgers University Press, 1985) looks at this cult from various perspectives.

Scientology has a great many hostile publications relating to it. The best scientific analysis is that of Roy Wallis, *The Road to Total Freedom* (New York, Columbia University Press, 1976). See also his article, "Societal Reaction to Scientology," in his edited book *Sectarianism* (London, Peter Owen, 1975), pp. 86–116. For a more slanted approach see Christopher Evans, *Cults of Unreason* (New York, Dell, 1973). From the same publishing company there is George Malko, *Scientology: The Now Religion* (1970).

The best introduction to the Divine Light cult is that of James V.

Downton, Jr., *Sacred Journeys: The Conversion of Young Americans to the Divine Light Mission* (New York, Columbia University Press, 1976). For some more specialized approaches the reader should consult Jeanne Messer, "Guru Maharaji Ji and the Divine Light Mission," in the Glock and Bellah volume previously cited, pp. 52–72; and Maeve Price, "The Divine Light Mission as a Social Organization," in *Sociological Review,* *27:*279–296, 1979.

Chapter 3

Demographic aspects of cults are discussed in Willa Appel, *Cults in America* (New York, Holt, Rinehart, and Winston, 1983); and in Rodney Stark and William Sims Bainbridge, *The Future of Religion* (Berkeley, University of California Press, 1985). Notions as to why people join cults is derived from the following works: Harvey Cox, *Turning East* (New York, Simon and Schuster, 1977); Philip E. Slater, *The Pursuit of Loneliness* (Boston, Beacon Press, 1971); J. Gordon Melton and Robert L. Moore, *The Cult Experience* (New York, Pilgrim Press, 1982); Charles Y. Glock, "The Role of Deprivation in the Origin and Evolution of Religious Groups," in Robert Lee and Martin Marty (Eds.), *Religion and Social Conflict* (New York, Oxford University Press, 1964), pp. 24–36; and the Appel volume previously cited.

Specific studies which have data on who joins and why they do so are: James V. Downton, Jr., *Sacred Journeys: The Conversion of Young Americans to the Divine Light Mission* (New York, Columbia University Press, 1976). For nice comparative data see also Francine Danner, "Conversion to Krishna Consciousness," in Roy Wallis (Ed.), *Sectarianism* (London, Peter Owen, 1975), pp. 53–69. For Bo and Peep, see Robert Balch and David Taylor, "Salvation in a UFO," in *Psychology Today, 10:*361–366, 1976, and their article, "Seekers and Saucers: The Role of the Cultic Milieu in Joining a UFO Cult," in *American Behavioral Scientist, 20:*839–860, 1977. Robert W. Balch has also focused on defection from this cult in "When the Light Goes Out, Darkness Comes," in Rodney Stark (Ed.), *Religious Movements* (New York, Paragon House, 1985), pp. 11–59. This excellent book also has other articles on joining and leaving cults and on changes in cults.

For the Meher Baba cult, consult the following: Tom Robbins, "Eastern Mysticism and the Resocialization of Drug Users," in *Journal for the Scientific Study of Religion, 8:*308–317, 1969; Thomas Robbins and Dick Anthony, "Getting Straight With Meher Baba," in their edited book, *In*

Gods We Trust (New Brunswick, Transaction Books, 1981), pp. 191–213, as well as their article, "The Meher Baba Movement: Its Effect on Post-Adolescent Social Alienation," in Irving I. Zaretsky and Mark P. Leone (Eds.), *Religious Movements in Contemporary America* (Princeton, Princeton University Press, 1974), pp. 479–511. See also section 3 in Jacob Needleman, *The New Religions* (Garden City, Doubleday, 1970).

Chapter 4

Willa Appel talks about the process of conversion in her book *Cults In America* (New York, Holt, Rinehart, and Winston, 1983). The basic model employed in this chapter is based on John Lofland and Rodney Stark, "Becoming a World-Saver: A Theory of Conversion to a Deviant Perspective," in *American Sociological Review, 30:*862–875, 1965. Along these lines, also see Max Heirich, "Changing Heart: A Test of Some Widely Held Theories About Religious Conversion," in *American Journal of Sociology, 83:*653–680, 1977, and Frederick R. Lynch, "Towards a Theory of Conversion and Commitment to the Occult," in *American Behavioral Scientist, 20:*887–907, 1977. The theoretical literature on this topic is enormous! A reader of value is James T. Richardson (Ed.), *Conversion Careers* (Beverly Hills, Sage, 1979).

On the aspects of Moonie conversion and on this cult in general, consult John Lofland, *Doomsday Cult* (Englewood Cliffs, Prentice-Hall, 1966); David Bromley and Anson D. Shupe, Jr., *Moonies In America* (Beverly Hills, Sage, 1979); and Frederick Sontag, *Sun Myung Moon and the Unification Church* (Nashville, Abingdon Press, 1977). An interesting approach is taken in Eileen Barker, *The Making of a Moonie: Choice or Brainwashing* (New York, Blackwell, 1984).

For the various steps to commitment, see Luther P. Gerlach and Virginia Hine, *People, Power, Change* (New York, Bobbs-Merrill, 1970) and Rosabeth Moss Kanter, *Commitment and Community* (Cambridge, Harvard University Press, 1972) for what makes it successful.

Responses to cults on various levels is generally discussed in David G. Bromley and Anson D. Shupe, *Strange Gods: The Great American Cult Scare* (Boston, Beacon Press, 1981) and in J. Gordon Melton, *Encyclopedic Handbook of Cults in America* (New York, Garland, 1986). See also James A. Beckford, *Cult Controversies* (London, Tavistock, 1985) and his more specific article, "A Typology of Family Responses to a New Religious Movement," in *Marriage and Family Review, 4:*41–55, 1981.

The brainwashing controversy has also generated a very large body of writings, pro and con. In general, I follow J. Gordon Melton and Robert L. Moore, *The Cult Experience* (New York, Pilgrim Press, 1982). For the first-person accounts, see Christopher Evans, *Crazy for God* (Englewood Cliffs, Prentice-Hall, 1979); Ted Patrick and Tom Dulak, *Let Our Children Go* (New York, Ballantine Books, 1976); and Barbara and Betty Underwook, *Hostage to Heaven* (New York, Potter, 1979). Anson D. Shupe and David Bromley discuss this issue in the *Strange Gods* book previously cited and in *The New Vigilantes: Deprogramers, Anti-Cultists and the New Religions* (Beverly Hills, Sage, 1980). A popular discussion is Margaret T. Singer, "Coming Out of the Cults," in *Psychology Today, 12:*72–82, 1979. A final and very interesting approach to reactions towards cults that impacts on this brainwashing controversy is that of the afore-mentioned Shupe and Bromley in an article by them, "Witches, Moonies, and Accusations of Evil," in Thomas Robbins and Dick Anthony (Eds.), *In Gods We Trust* (New Brunswick, Transaction Books, 1981), pp. 247–261. It is difficult to arrive at conclusions in these matters.

Chapter 5

The classic work in anthropology on cult development is that of Anthony F. C. Wallace, "Revitalization Movements," in *American Anthropologist, 58:*264–281, 1956. The excellent book by Rodney Stark and William Sims Bainbridge previously cited, *The Future of Religion* (Berkeley, University of California Press, 1985) contains several chapters which bear on how cults develop and become successful. It also includes the discussion of the career of Transcendental Meditation. This specific cult is also described briefly in J. Gordon Melton, *Encyclopedic Handbook of Cults in America* (New York, Graland, 1986). A popular expression is John White, *Everything You Want To Know About TM* (New York, Pocket Books, 1976). The general volume by Luther Gerlach and Virginia Hine, *People, Power, Change* (New York, Bobbs-Merrill, 1970) also speaks to the supra-individual levels of cult growth and development.

The interested student would profit at this point by reading something specific on cult growth, change, failure, and related topics. Two excellent examples which also bring up other issues are a cult that was derived from Scientology but underwent a complex series of changes and the People's Temple Movement of Jim Jones. The former is related in William Sims Bainbridge, *Satan's Power* (Berkeley, University of California Press, 1978). The road to Jonestown and disaster is documented on many levels and from different points of view. A very popular treatment is Marshall Kilduff and Ron James, *The Suicide Cult* (New York, Bantam Books, 1978). A historical view is supplied by Tim Reiterman, *Raven: The Untold Story of The Rev. Jim Jones and His People* (New York, Dutton, 1982). A collection of articles on this cult, some of which generalize to others, is Ken Levi (Ed.), *Violence and Religious Commitment* (University Park, Pennsylvania State University Press, 1982).

Students of cult development, recognizing that mainline faiths often begin as cults, should also read on the early stages of the history of major faiths such as Buddhism and Christianity to gain insights into these matters.

Chapter 6

Willa Appel's scheme is suggested in her book, *Cults in America* (New York, Holt, Rinehart, and Winston, 1983). Geoffrey K. Nelson has examined cults theoretically in his article, "The Concept of Cult," *Sociological Review, 16:*351–362, 1968. Accounts of the Church Of All Worlds and a number of related experiments are found in Margot Adler, *Drawing Down The Moon* (Boston, Beacon Press, 1986). The book, *The Future of Religion,* by Rodney Stark and William Sims Bainbridge (Berkeley, University of California Press, 1985) contains the classification of audience cults, client cults, and cult movements. The Amalgamated Flying Saucer Clubs of America is discussed in Robert S. Ellwood, Jr., *Religious and Spiritual Groups in Modern America* (Englewood Cliffs, Prentice-Hall, 1988). An article which details the lure of such cults is that by H. T. Buckner, "The Flying Saucerians: An Open Door Cult," found in Marcello Truzzi (Ed.), *Sociology and Everyday Life* (Englewood Cliffs, Prentice-Hall, 1968). The most interesting example of a UFO type cult is the Aetherius Society, discussed by Roy Wallis in his book *Sectarianism* (London, Peter Owen, 1975).

Bryan R. Wilson's most accessible presentation of his typology is in his book, *Magic and the Millennium* (New York, Harper and Row, 1973). This work illustrates the scheme with examples from tribal and third-world peoples. For a discussion of its usefulness in more modern societies, see Michael R. Welch, "Analyzing Religious Sects: An Empirical Examination of Wilson's Sect Typology," in *Journal for the Scientific Study of Religion, 16:*125–139, 1977.

For an introduction to Christian Science and the Christadelphians, examples cited for Wilson's scheme not covered in the present text, consult the following: *The Emergence of Christian Science in American*

Religious Life by Stephen Gottschalk (Berkeley, University of California Press, 1978) and Charles S. Braden, *Christian Science Today* (Dallas, Southern Methodist University Press, 1958). For the Christadelphians, consult Bryan R. Wilson, *Sects and Society* (Berkeley, University of California Press, 1961). This also contains material on Christian Science. A brief account of the Oneida community is given in William M. Kephart, *Extraordinary Groups* (New York, St. Martin's Press, 1987). This book also includes a description of the Amish. The best book on these people is John A. Hostetler, *Amish Society* (Baltimore, Johns Hopkins Press, 1980).

A general and classic book on primitive cults is by Vittorio Lanternari, *The Religions of the Oppressed* (New York, Knopf, 1963). I have selected three anthropological examples of cult schemes from among the many that exist. The sources for these are: Ralph Linton, "Nativistic Movements," in *American Anthropologist, 45:*230–240, 1943; Marian W. Smith, "Towards a Classification of Cult Movements," in *Man, 51:*8–12, 1959; and David F. Aberle, *The Peyote Religion Among The Navaho* (Chicago, Aldine, 1966). For two contrasting schemes, the reader might consult Simone Clemhout, "Typology of Nativistic Movements," in *Man, 64:*14–15, 1964, and Igor Kopytoff, "Classifications of Religious Movements: Analytical and Synthetic," in June Helm (Ed.), *Symposium in New Approaches to the Study of Religion* (Seattle, University of Washington Press, 1964), pp. 77–90.

Chapter 7

The selection of religious movements to illustrate the frustrations of Native North Americans is somewhat arbitrary. Readers interested in more details on cults mentioned in this chapter should consult the following works. The classic work on the Ghost Dance is James Mooney, *The Ghost Dance Religion and the Sioux Outbreak of 1890* (Chicago, University of Chicago Press, 1965, orig. 1896). For earlier manifestations and influences, see Leslie Spier, *The Ghost Dance of 1970 Among the Klamath of Oregon* (University of Washington Publications In Anthropology *2:*39–56, 1927) and Cora DuBois, "The 1870 Ghost Dance," in *Anthropological Records,* (University of California Press, 1939, vol. 3). For historical influences, see Leslie Spier, *The Prophet Dance of the Northwest and its Derivatives: The Source of the Ghost Dance* (Menasha, George Banta, 1935). Alexander Lesser, "Cultural Significance of the Ghost Dance," in *American Anthropologist, 35:*108–115, 1933, suggests how some revitalization and return to the past did occur.

The Smohalla cult is discussed in the Mooney work cited above and by

Click Relander, *Drummers And Dreamers* (Coldwell, Caxton Press, 1956). For the Handsome Lake movement, see Anthony F. C. Wallace, *The Death and Rebirth of the Seneca* (New York, Knopf, 1970). This book places the cult in an overall context of deprivation and revitalization. See also Merle H. Deardorff, "The Religion of Handsome Lake: Its Origins and Development," in *Symposium on Local Diversity in Iroquois Culture,* (Bureau of American Ethnology Bulletin 149, 1951) and Arthur C. Parker, *The Code of Handsome Lake* (New York State Museum Bulletin 163, 1912).

The Peyote cult has been surveyed in grand fashion by Weston LaBarre in *The Peyote Cult* (New Haven, Yale University Press, 1938) (and in recent editions). The Taos materials are taken from my own work on that cult: "A Descriptive Introduction to the Taos Peyote Ceremony," in *Ethnology,* 7:427–449, 1968, and "Peyotism and Religious Membership at Taos Pueblo, New Mexico," in *Southwestern Social Science Quarterly,* 48: 183–191, 1967. Two books are invaluable for a complete picture on this cult: S. J. Slotkin, *The Peyote Religion* (Glencoe, Free Press, 1956) summarizes much of this author's work on this cult and Omer C. Stewart, *Peyote Religion* (Norman, University of Oklahoma Press, 1987) gives an historical perspective.

For a selection of other Native American cults, consult Verne F. Ray, "The Kolaskin Cult," in *American Anthropologist,* 38:67–75, 1936; Homer G. Barnett, *Indian Shakers: A Messianic Cult of the Pacific Northwest* (Carbondale, Southern Illinois Press, 1957); and for one that spawned much military resistance, that of the Shawnee prophet Tenskwatawa, consult R. David Edmunds, *The Shawnee Prophet* (Lincoln, University of Nebraska Press, 1983).

Two general volumes dealing with Caribbean and South American cults are Roger Bastide, *The African Religions of Brazil* (Baltimore, Johns Hopkins Press, 1978) and George Eaton Simpson, *Black Religions in the New World* (New York, Columbia University Press, 1978). For the three specific cult examples cited in this chapter, consult the following: Donald Hogg, "The Convince Cult of Jamaica," in *Yale University Publications in Anthropology,* 58:3–24, 1960; Migene Gonzalez-Wippler, *Santeria: African Magic in Latin America* (New York, Doubleday, 1975); Sheila Kitzinger, "Protest and Mysticism: The Rastafari Cult of Jamaica," in *Journal for the Scientific Study of Religion,* 8:247–251, 1969; and Leonard E. Barrett, *The Rastafarians* (London, Heinemann, 1977).

Many other cults exist in these areas and the interested reader may wish to consult the following very rich accounts: Seth and Ruth Leacock,

Spirits of the Deep (Garden City, Doubleday, 1972) (on the Batuque of Brazil) and Alfred Metraux, *Voodoo in Haiti* (New York, Oxford University Press, 1959).

Chapter 8

There is a large anthropological literature on cults among tribal peoples in the Pacific Islands and only a small portion can be cited here. The interested reader would do best to consult Peter Worsley, *The Trumpet Shall Sound* (New York, Schocken Books, 1968), which is a classic general survey for Melanesian examples. A more recent and restricted study is by Glynn Cochrane, *Big Men and Cargo Cults* (Oxford, Clarendon Press, 1970). See also two books by Kenelem Burridge: *New Heaven, New Earth* (New York, Schocken Books, 1969) and a more specific study, *Mambu* (New York, Harper and Row, 1960). These books also suggest theoretical aspects for such religious movements. For the theoretically minded see also I. C. Jarvie, "Theories of Cargo Cults: A Critical Analysis," in *Oceania, 34:* 1–31, 109–136, 1963, which surveys much of the literature up to that point.

The specific examples used in the present chapter are also discussed in the following accounts: F. E. Williams, "The Vailala Madness and the Destruction of Native Ceremonies in the Gulf Division," *Papuan Anthropological Reports,* Number 4, 1919, and Roger M. Keesing, "Politico-Religious Movements and Anti-Colonialism on Malaita: Maasina Rule in Historical Perspective," in *Oceania, 48:* 241–261, and *49:* 46–73, 1978. For the Hau Hau, Polynesian example, see S. B. Babbage, *Hau Hauism* (Wellington, Reed, 1937); William Greenwood, "The Upraised Hand," in *Journal of the Polynesian Society, 51:* 1–81, 1942; and Robin W. Winks, "The Doctrine of Hau Hauism," in the same journal, *62:* 199–236, 1953. For a comparative movement in Polynesia, see J. D. Freeman, "The Joe Gimlet or Siovili Cult," in *Anthropology of the South Seas* (New Plymouth, Avery, 1971), pp. 185–198.

Several volumes exist on Japanese religious movements. Perhaps the two best are Harry Thomsen, *The New Religions of Japan* (Tokyo, Tuttle, 1963) and H. Neil McFarland, *The Rush Hour of the Gods* (New York, Collier-MacMillan, 1967). Robert S. Ellwood, Jr. does his usual masterful job in discussing some of these which are spreading to the United States in *The Eagle and the Rising Sun* (Philadelphia, Westminster Press, 1974). See also C. B. Offner and H. Van Straelen, *Modern Japanese Religions* (Leiden, E. J. Brill, 1963). The chapter examples are mainly paraphrased from the above works, but also see H. Van Straelin, *The Religion of Divine Wisdom* (Kyoto, Veritos Shoin, 1957). For in-depth treatment of specific cases not covered in this chapter, see Winston Davis, *Dojo: Magic and Exorcism in Modern Japan* (Stanford, Stanford University Press, 1980) (for Sukyo Mahikari/true light suprareligious organization) and James W. White, *The Soka Gakkai And Mass Society* (same publisher, 1970). This very political religion is also discussed by James Allen Dator, "The Soka Gakkai: A Sociological Interpretation," in *Contemporary Religions in Japan,* 6:205–242, 1965.

James W. Fernandez has written two articles on the classification of African cults. Both are titled "African Religious Movements." One that deals mainly with classification is in the *Journal of African Studies, 2:*531–549, 1964. The other, which raises more issues in the study of such phenomena, is in the *Annual Review of Anthropology, 7:*195–234, 1978. For the specific cults described in this chapter, I have used the following accounts: Johannes Fabian, *Jamaa: A Charismatic Movement in Katanga* (Evanston, Northwestern University Press, 1971); James W. Fernandez, "Symbolic Consensus in a Fang Reformative Cult," in *American Anthropologist, 67:*902–927, 1965, deals with Bwiti and is especially good at pointing out the levels of knowledge possessed by cult members regarding symbolism and other matters. His more recent book, *Bwiti* (Princeton, Princeton University Press, 1982) explores varieties of this cult in great detail against the background of Fang culture and history. Finally, consult James B. Christensen, "The Tigari Cult of West Africa," in *Papers of the Michigan Academy of Science, Arts, and Letters, 39:*389–398, 1954.

Two other works provide interesting data on leaders and movements in Africa. First, the classic work by Bengst G. M. Sundkler, *Bantu Prophets in South Africa* (London, Oxford University Press, 1948) and then the more recent work by Wyatt MacGaffey, *Modern Kongo Prophets* (Bloomington, Indiana University Press, 1983). For a few other specific cases for comparative purposes, see J. D. Y. Peel, *Aladura: A Religious Movement Among the Yoruba* (London, Oxford University Press, 1968), and for a discussion of both book and movement, see Robin Horton, "African Conversions," in *Africa, 41:*85–108, 1971. Two other cult accounts are R. I. Rotberg, "The Lenshina Movement of Northern Rhodesia," in *Rhodes-Livingston Journal, 29:*63–78, 1961 (Aka the Lumpa Church) and John Middleton, "The Yakan or Allah Water Cult Among the Lugbara," in the *Journal of the Royal Anthropological Institute,* 93:80–108, 1963.

Chapter 9

The idea of "new consciousness" has aroused a host of comments and articles both as to the data on which it is based and in the scientific posture behind the concept. For a sample, the interested reader might begin with Robert Wuthnow, *The Consciousness Reformation* (Berkeley, University of California Press, 1976). Then read the articles by Robert N. Bellah, "New Religious Consciousness and the Crisis of Modernity," and Charles Y. Glock, "Consciousness Among Contemporary Youth: An Interpretation," both in *The New Religious Consciousness,* pp. 333–352 and 353–366, respectively. This volume, which they edited, was also published by the University of California Press in 1976. For a critique of the reality of this concept and of Wuthnow, see William Simms Bainbridge and Rodney Stark, "The Consciousness Reformation Reconsidered," in *Journal for the Scientific Study of Religion, 20:* 1–16, 1981, and Wuthnow's rejoiner in the same issue, "Two Traditions in the Study of Religion," pp. 16–32. A more recent use of the concept with a different data base is that of Angela A. Aidala, "World Views, Ideologies and Social Experimentation: Clarification and Replication of the Consciousness Reformation," also in *Journal for Scientific Study of Religion, 23:* 44–59, 1984. This is in general supportive of the concept and of Wuthnow, whose later article, "Religious Movements and Counter Movements in North America," in James A. Beckford (Ed.), *New Religious Movements and Rapid Social Change* (Berkeley Hills, Sage, 1986, pp. 1–28, is also valuable. This volume has a worldwide perspective and is most useful. Finally, an article by Steven M. Tipton, "Zen Practice and Moral Meaning," in Dick Anthony et al., *Spiritual Choices* (New York, Paragon House, 1987), pp. 211–231, also discusses styles of meaning/consciousness as influencing behavior in the United States.

The list of psychological coercion and deception characters is taken from Susan M. Anderson, "Identifying Coercion and Deception in Social Systems," in Brock K. Kilbourne (Ed.), *Scientific Research and New Religions* (San Francisco, American Association for the Advancement of Science Proceedings 2, part 2, 1985, pp. 12–22. Also consult Lita Linzer Schwartz, "Viewing the Cults: Differences of Opinion," pp. 149–158, in the same volume. The viewpoint from transpersonal psychology represented in this chapter is taken from an important collection of articles and discussions in Dick Anthony et al., *Spiritual Choices: The Problem of Recognizing Authentic Paths to Inner Transformation* (New York, Paragon

House, 1987). Specifically, consult Frances Vaughan, "A Question of Balance: Health and Pathology in New Religious Movements," pp. 265–280; and John Welwood, "On Spiritual Authority: Genuine and Counterfeit," pp. 283–300. Two other articles in this volume based upon specific schemes for cult evaluation are Dick Anthony and Bruce Ecker, "The Anthony Typology: A Framework of Assessing Spiritual and Consciousness Groups," pp. 35–105, which divides such groups up into eight potential types, with some having a greater potential for harmful aspects than others, and Ken Wilber, "The Spectrum Model," pp. 237–260. The latter assumes stages of personal psychological growth including levels of superconsciousness and evaluates groups in terms of the absence of rational elements and the mixing of levels resulting in problematic groups having "cult clans with totem masters." His work may be heavy going for the uninitiated. Somewhat more entertaining is Rick M. Chapman, *How to Choose a Guru* (New York, Harper and Row, 1973).

INDEX